Myths and Legends

Adult Coloring Book

Life is full of things that stress us out. Between work, children, bills, and chores at home, our minds are inundated with stuff vying for our attention. Coloring is a great way to relax and allow stress to melt away.

Have a problem you are trying to figure out? Just open up this book, take your colored pencils, and begin filling in the blank spaces. Don't focus on anything, but coloring what is within this book. By doing this, you will clear your mind, and just might come up with the solution you've been searching for.

With 30 designs to color, this book has something for every skill level. So just take a moment to relax and color.

You can tear this page out and use it to put between the images so as to avoid bleed through.

Pele

Hawaiian goddess of fire.

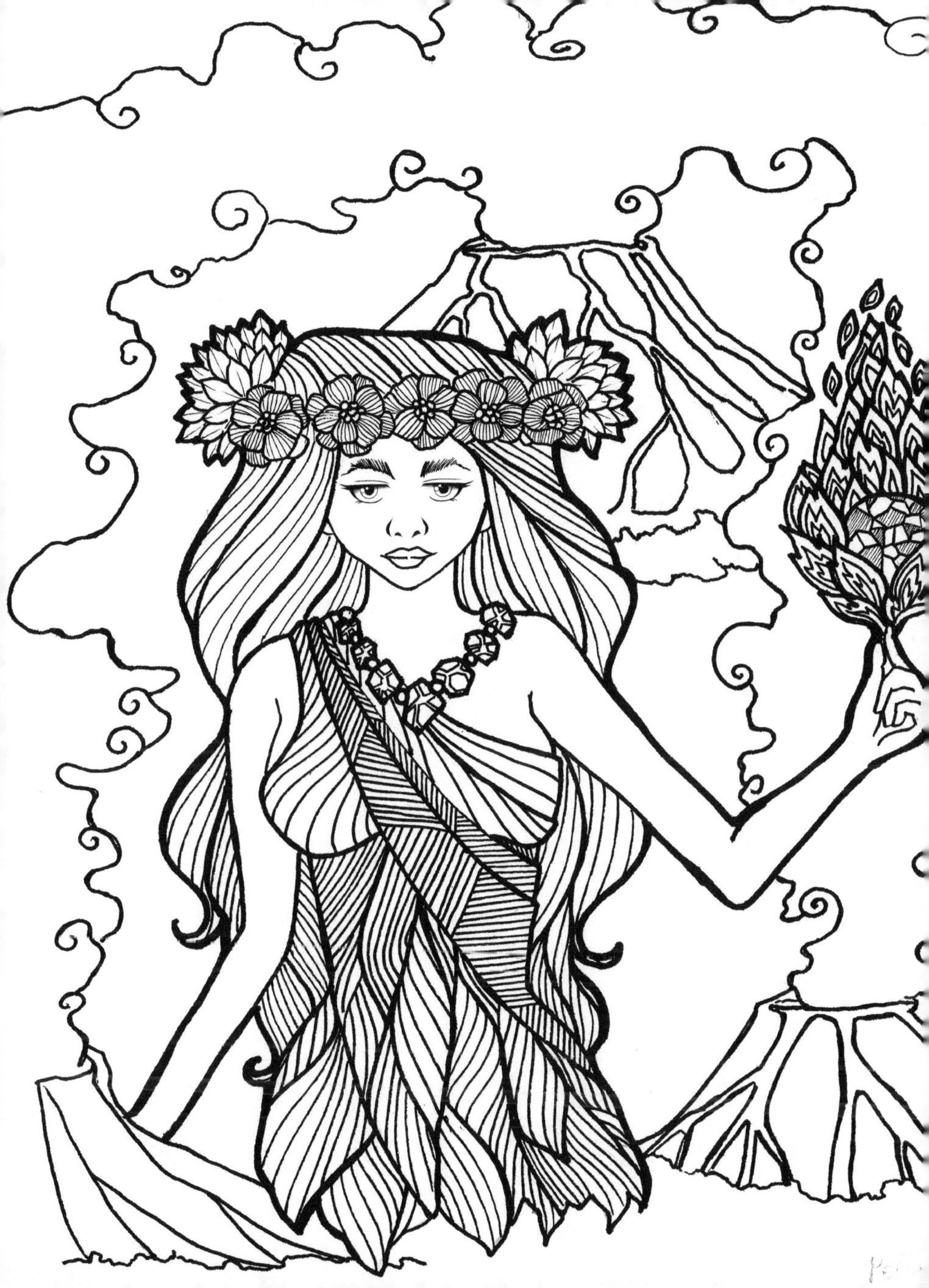

Thor

Norse god of thunder well-known for his quick
temper and weapon of choice: his hammer

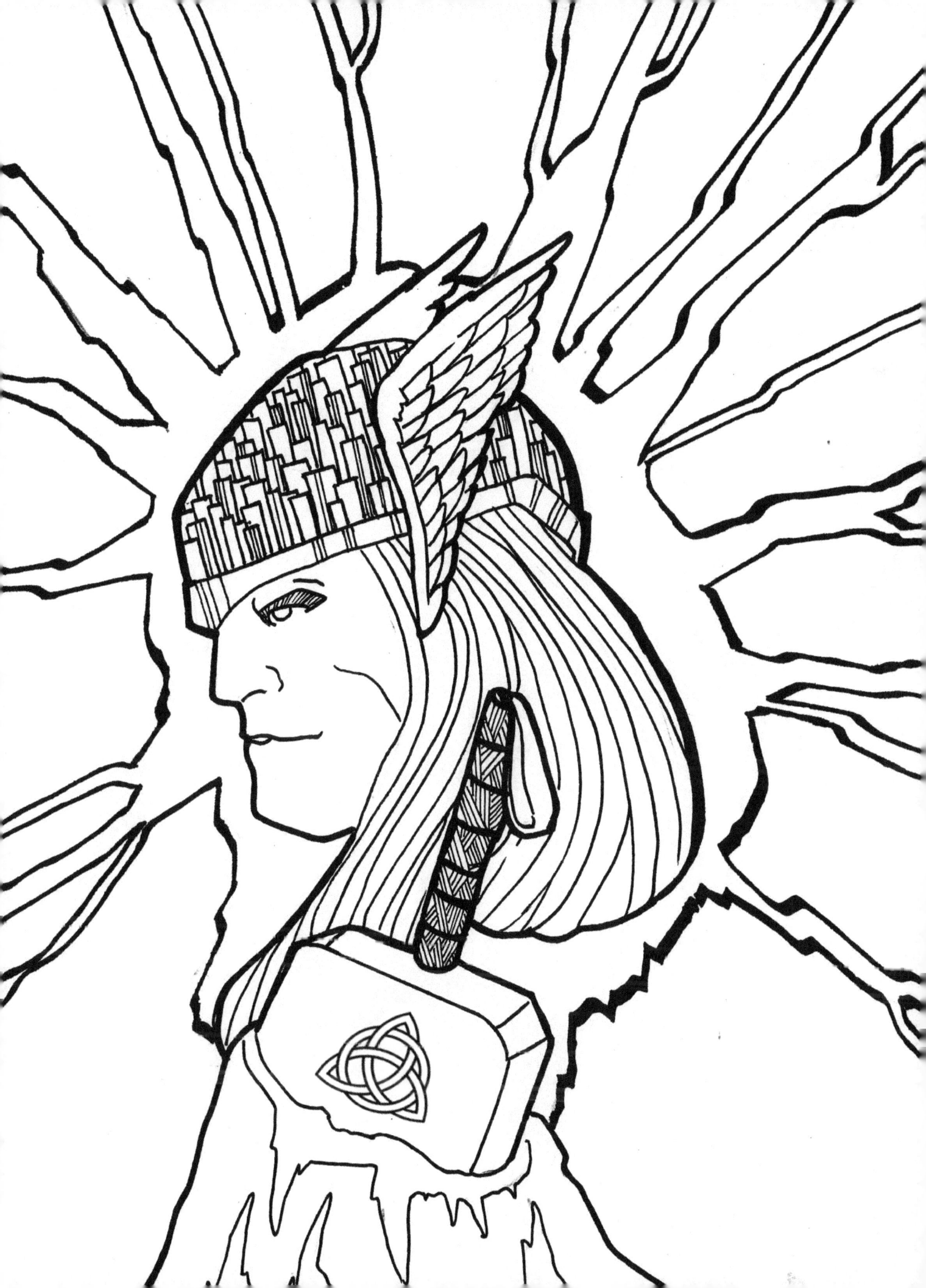

Freya

Norse Goddess of love, fertility, sex, beauty, and war.

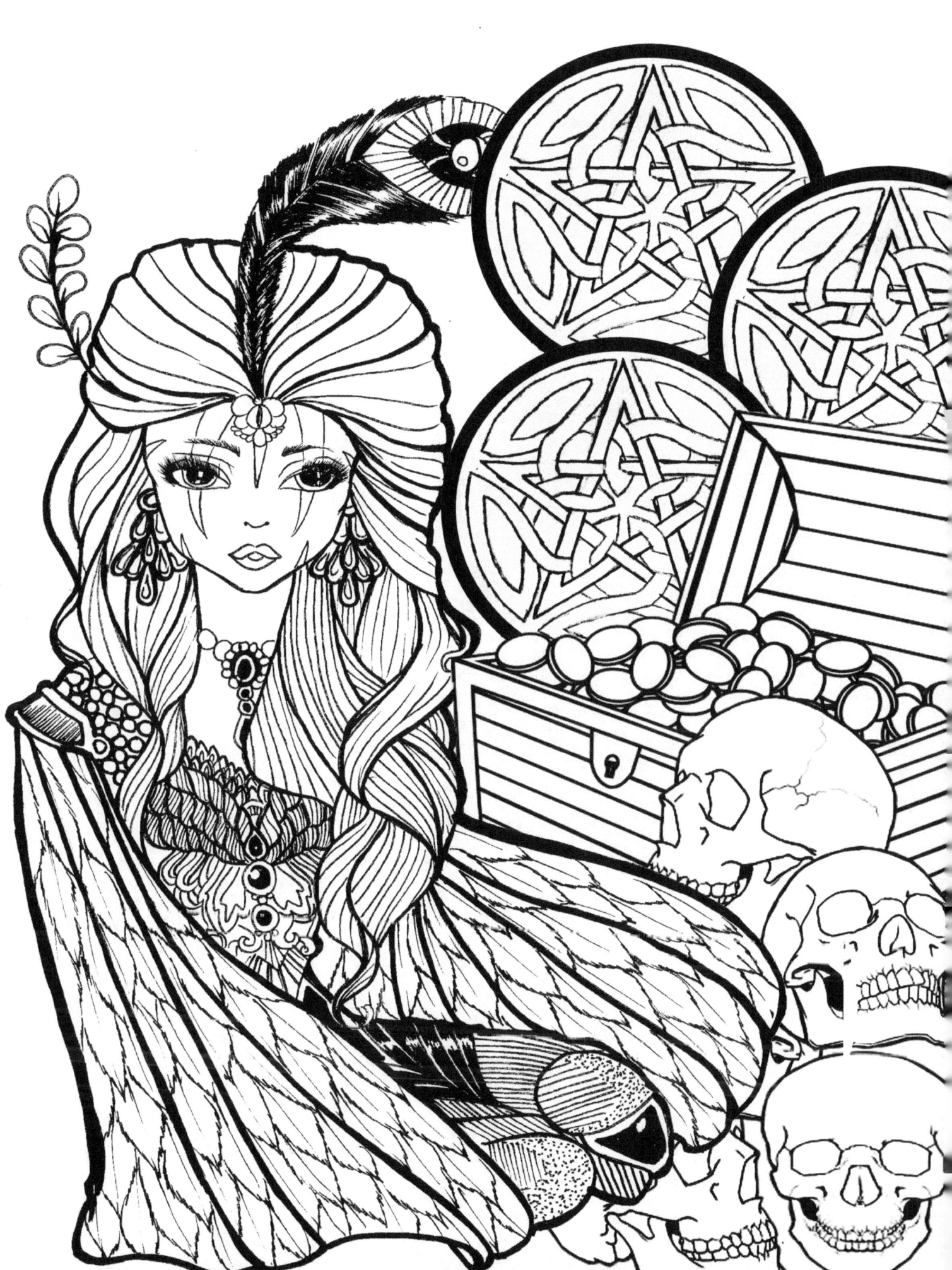

Isis

Protector of the dead and children and wife to Osiris.

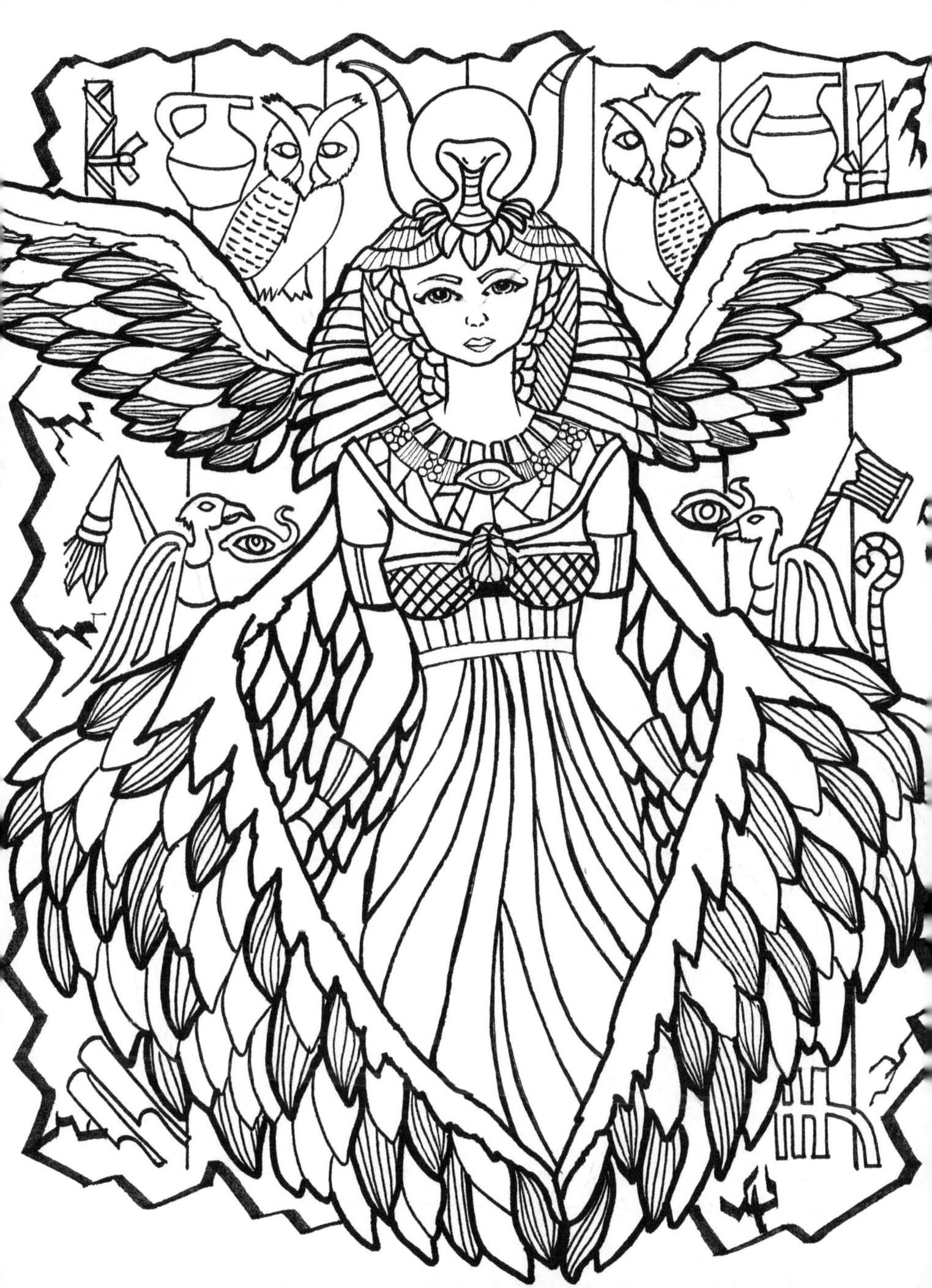

Aunty Greenleaf
and the
White Deer

A legend from New England. Aunty Greenleaf is
believed to be a witch and one best not crossed.

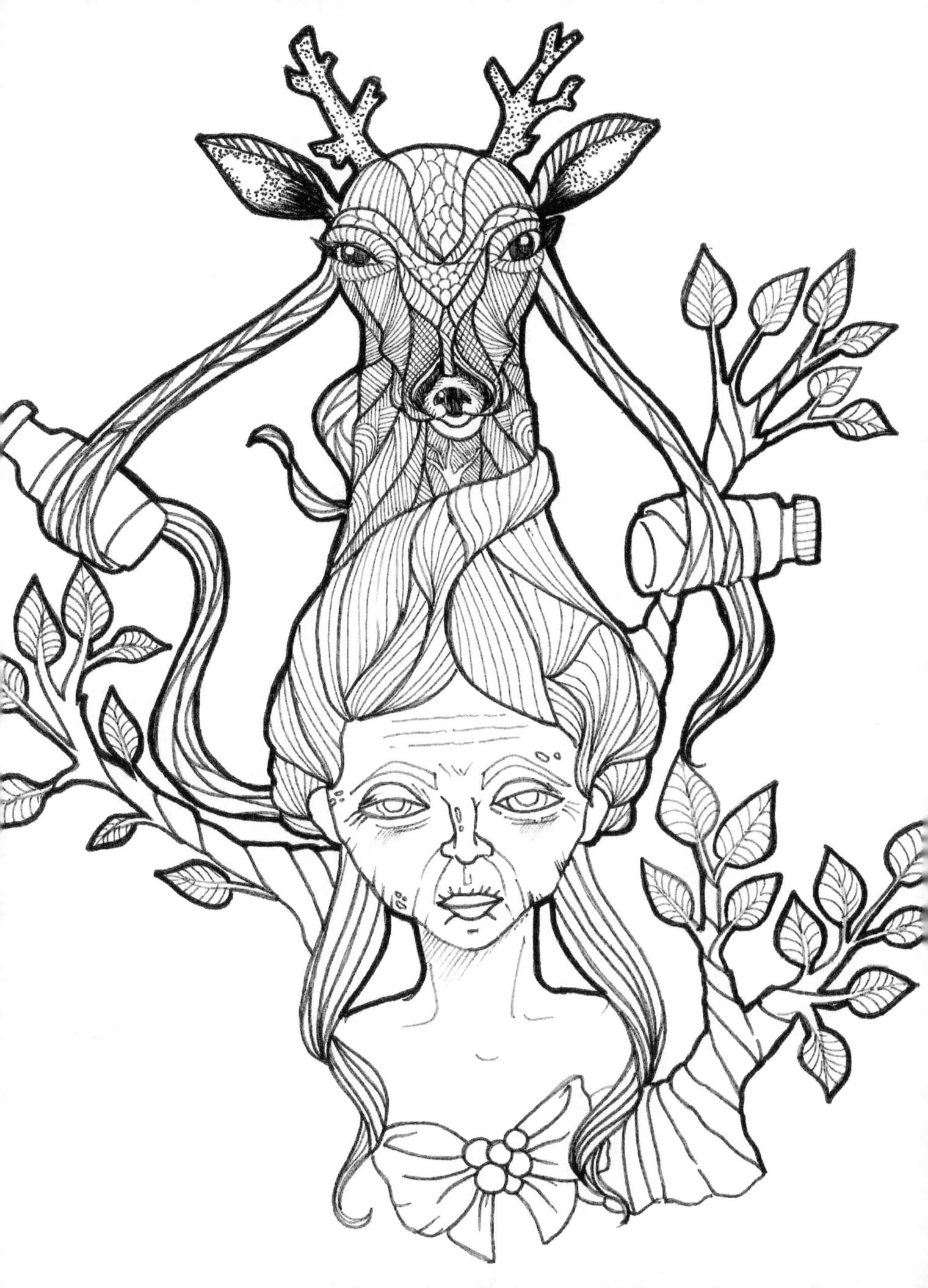

Bear Lake Monster

Supposedly it haunts Bear Lake in Utah, USA.

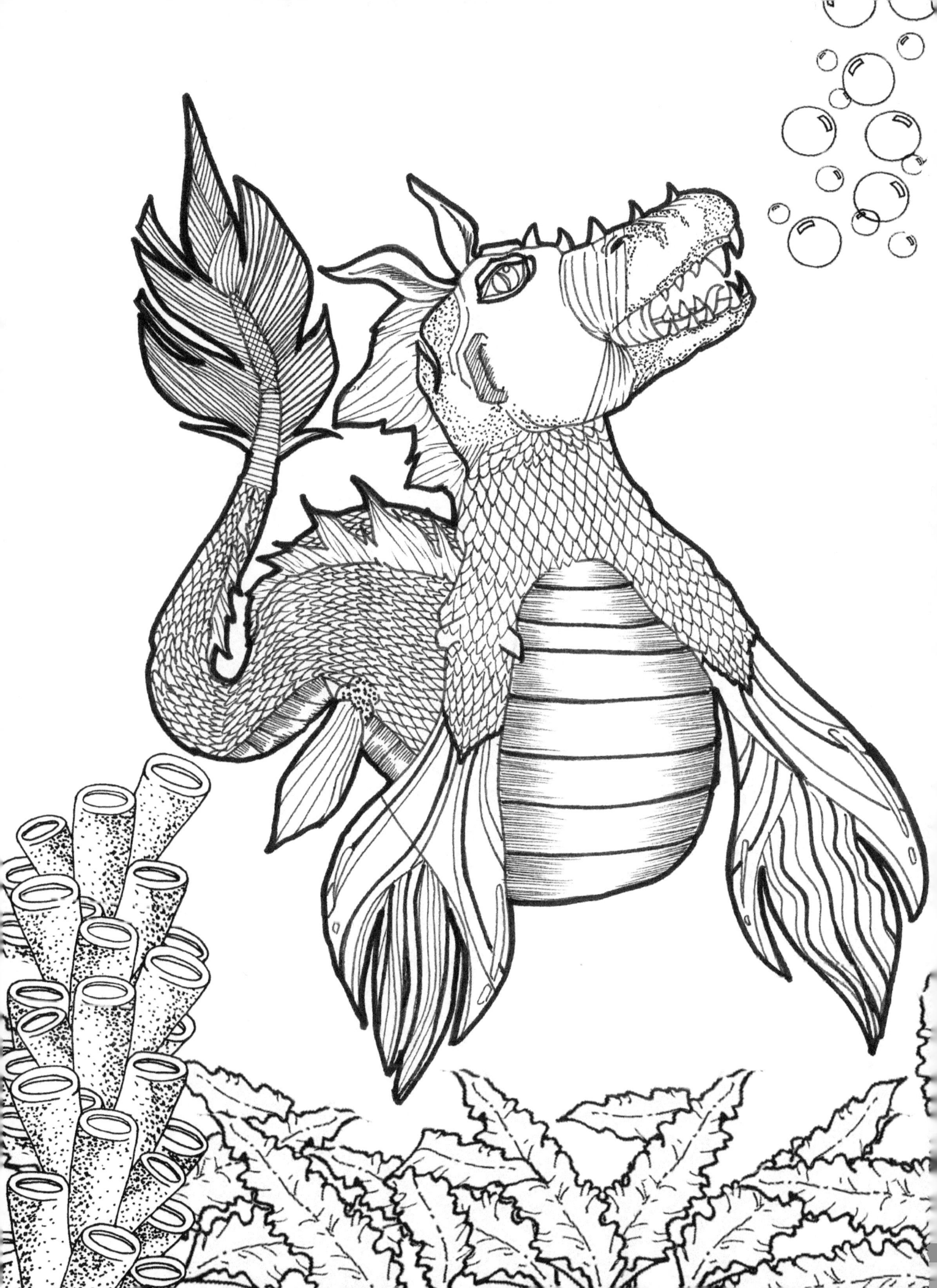

Blackbeard's Ghost

Blackbeard was an infamous pirate who terrorized sailors in Carribbean and the Atlantic. He was ruthless and unmerciful. It's rumored that his ghost still haunts the North Carolina (USA) coast.

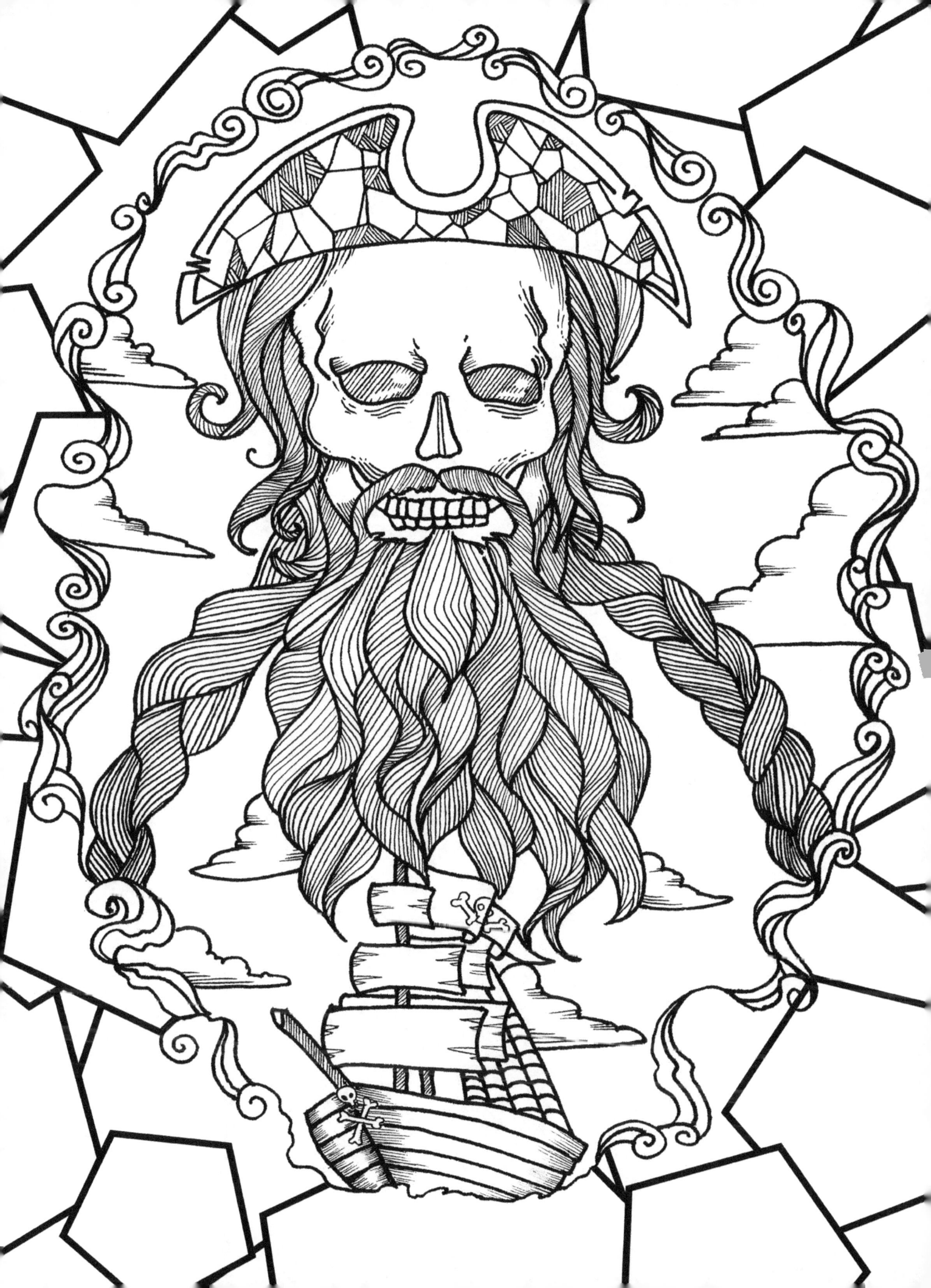

Abuk

From Sudanese mythology and is considered the patron goddess of women and gardens.

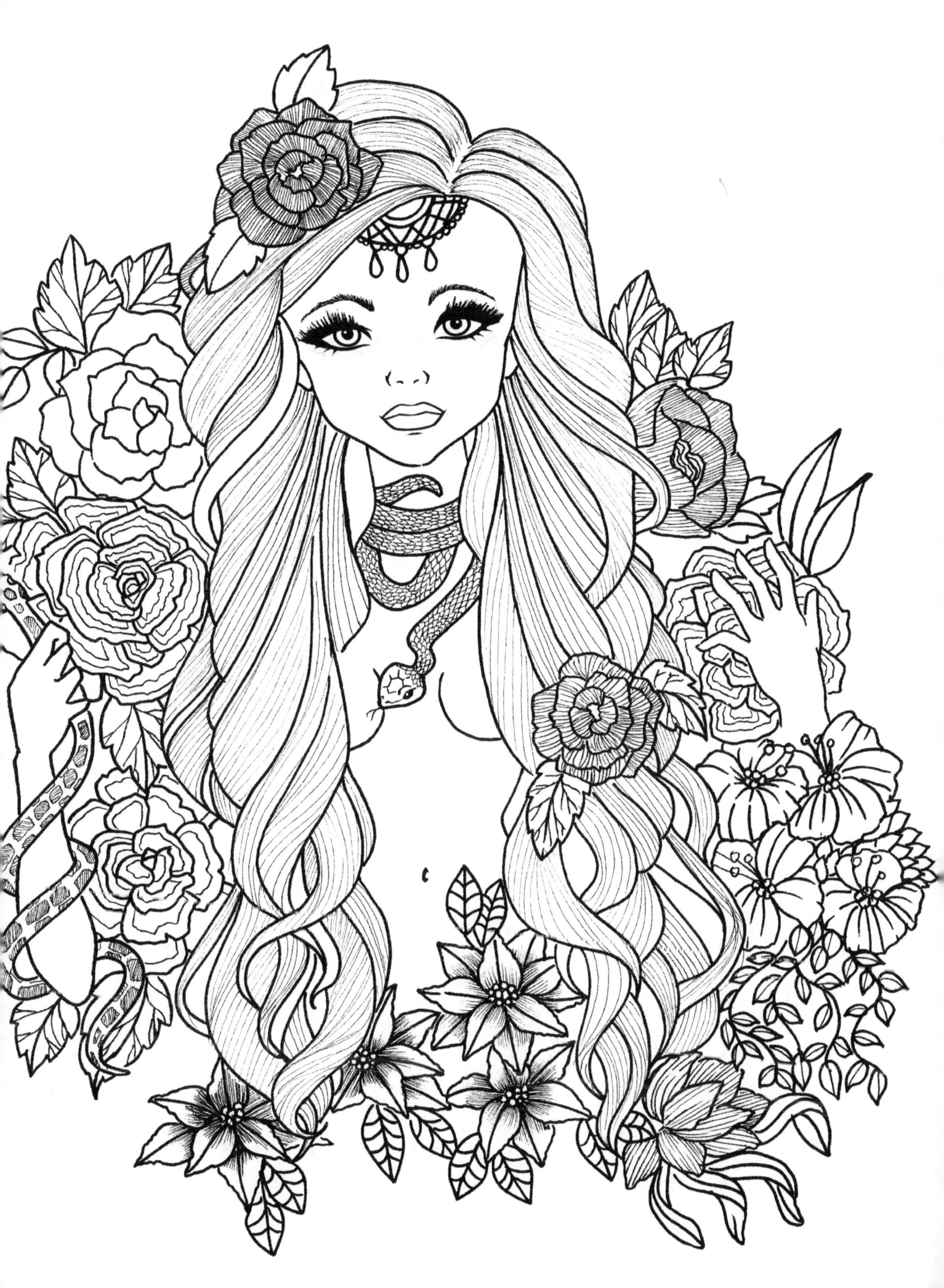

Mbaba Mwana Waresa

From Zulu mythology and is considered the patron
goddess of agriculture, the harvest, rain, and rainbows.

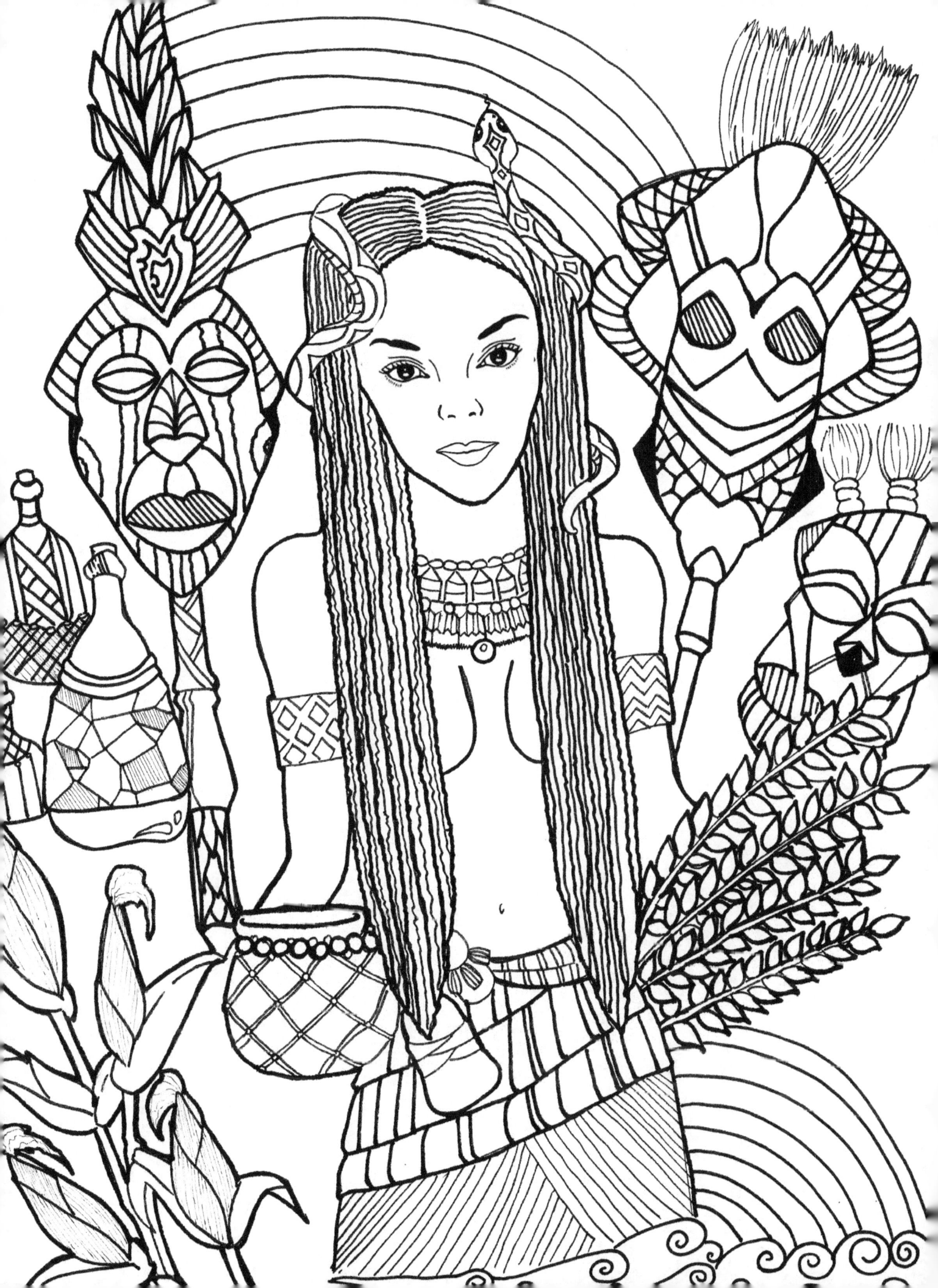

Mami Wata

A water spirit who is said to reside in Africa's
western coastal regions.

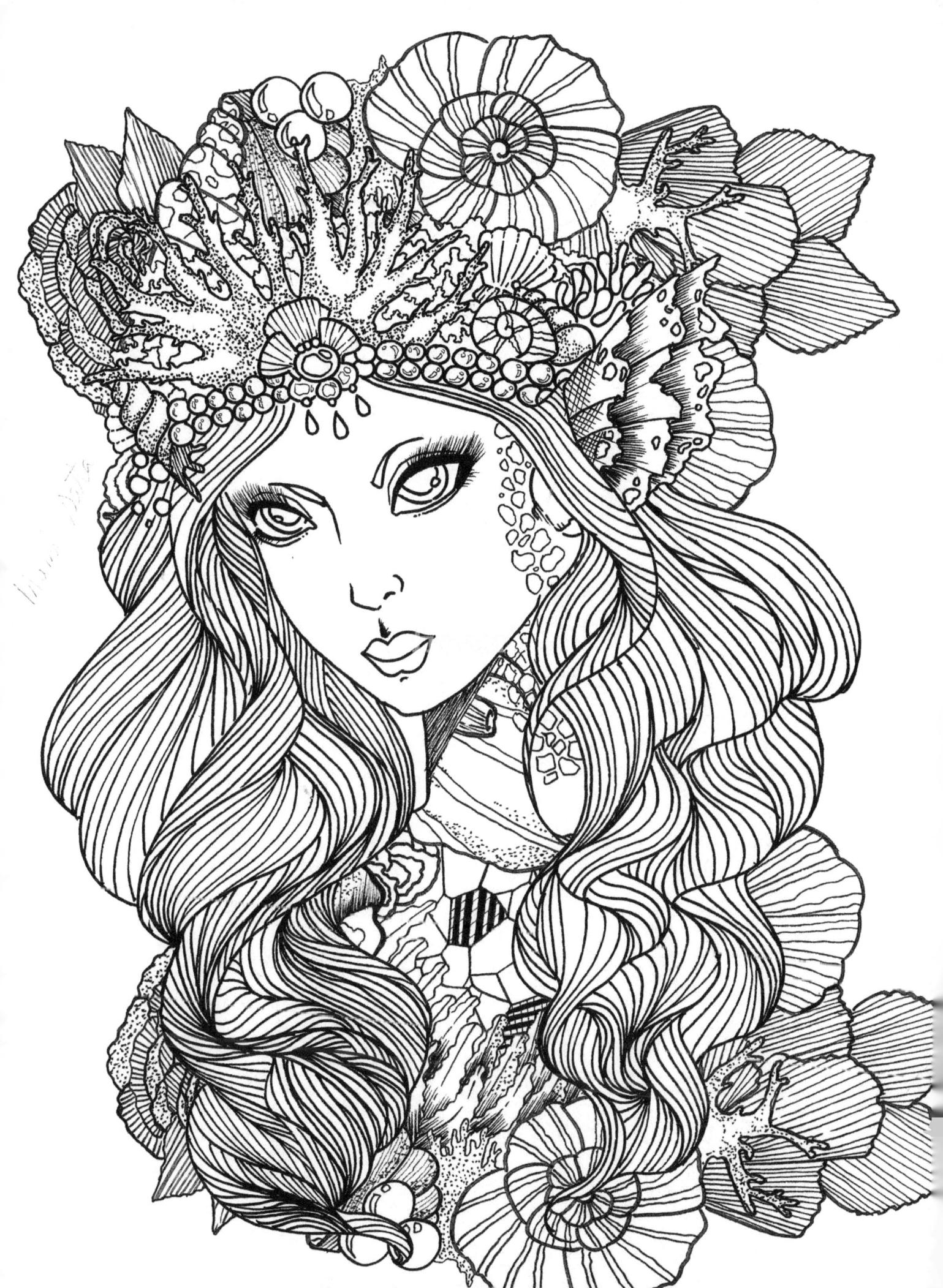

Manāt

The Meccan goddess of destiny. She is also believed
to be the goddess of fate and death.

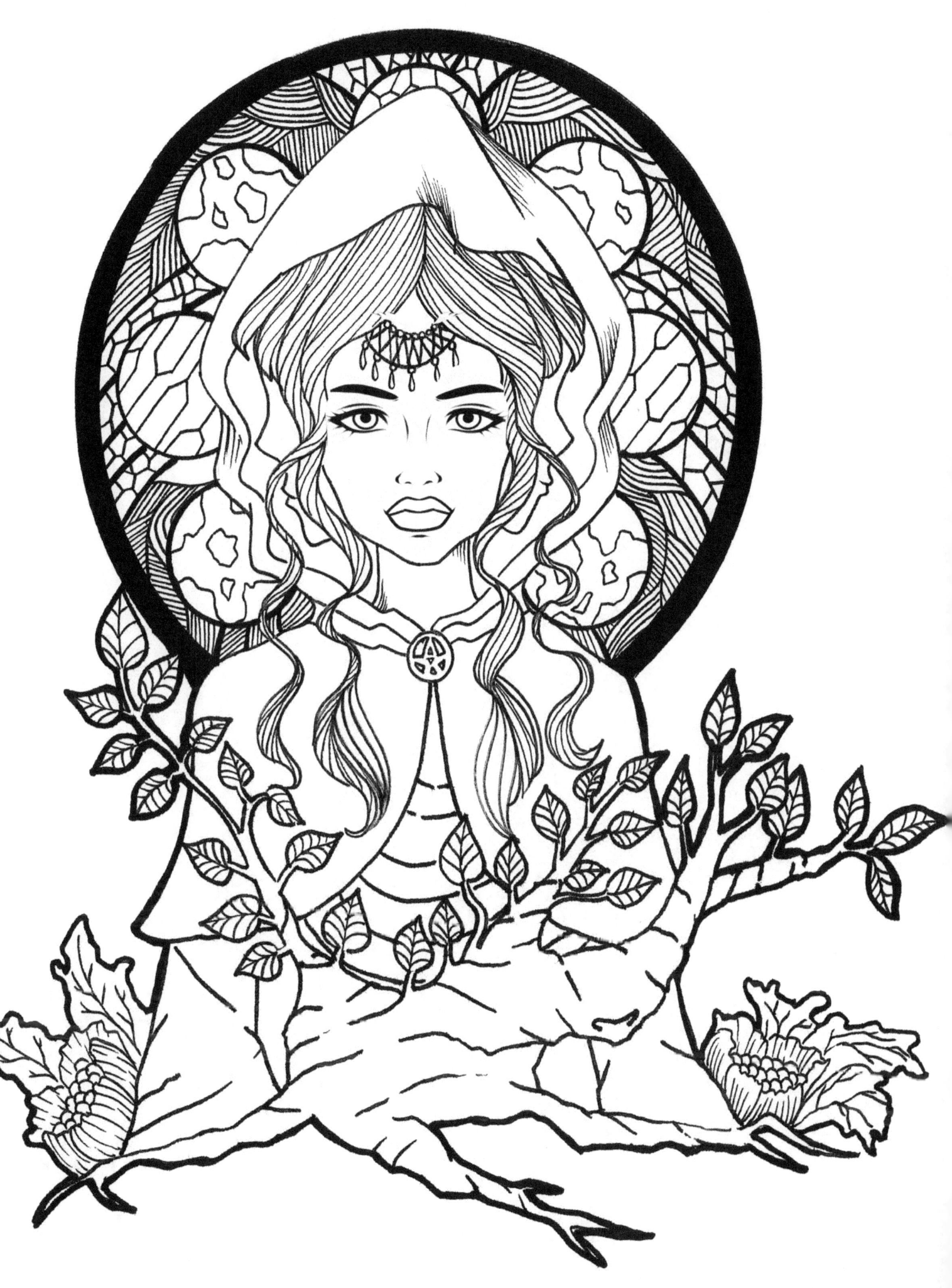

Erinle

Origin is Africa and is considered the god of health and wellness. It is also believed that he served as the physician of the other gods.

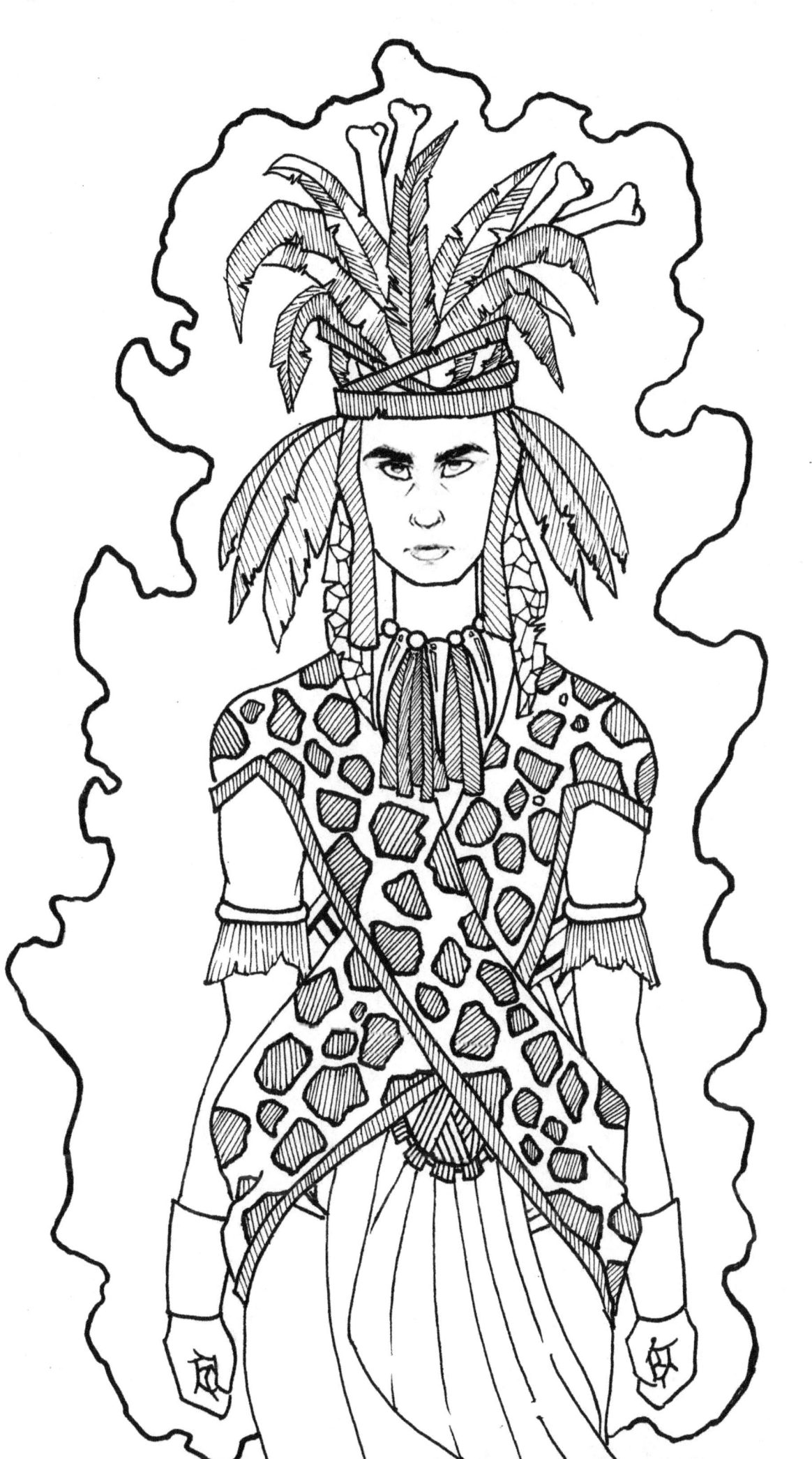

Esu

African in origin. Esu is considered a trickster god
and is also known as the god of crossroads.

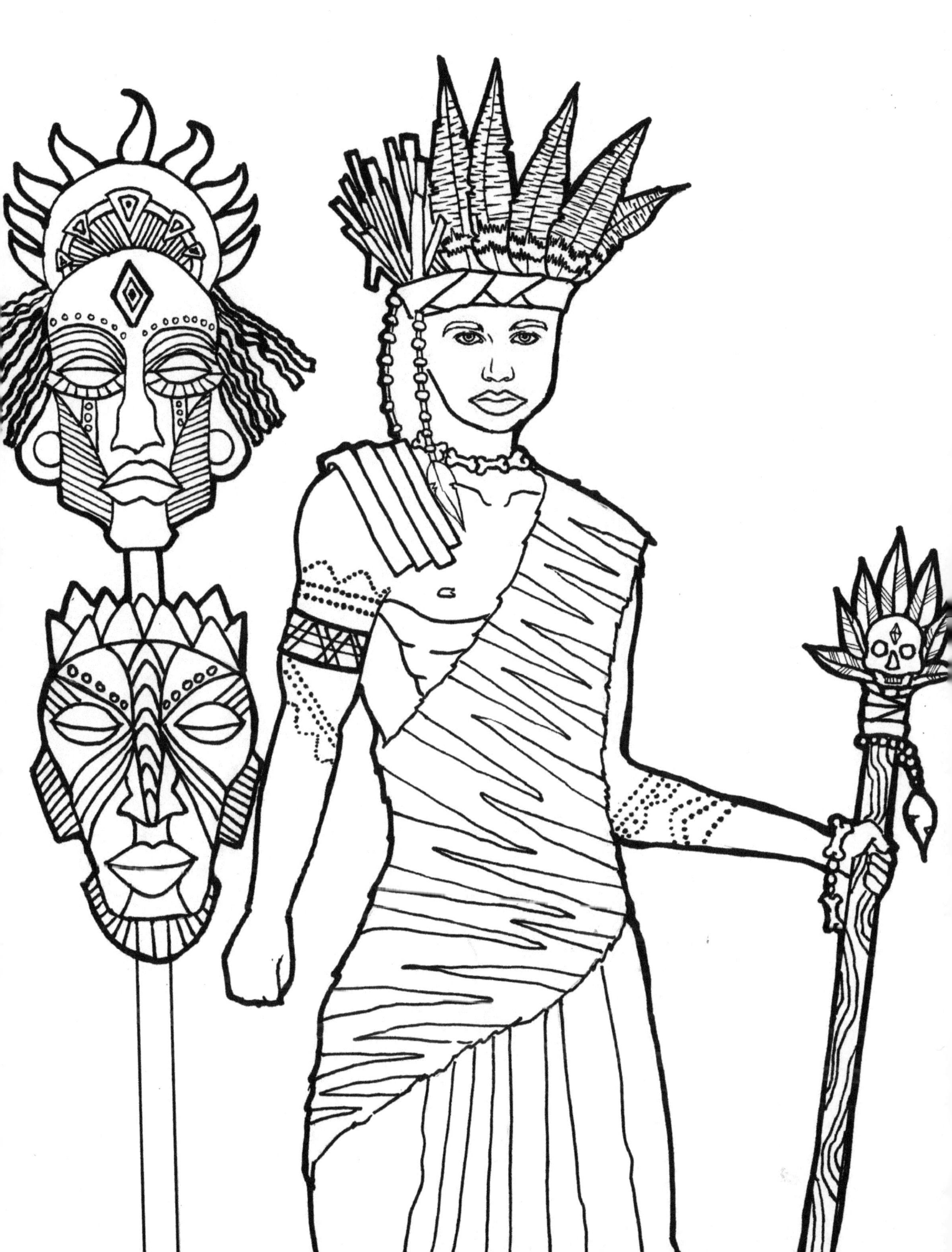

Elijah

A prophet from Hebrew mythology and believed to have been lifted into heaven in a fiery chariot.

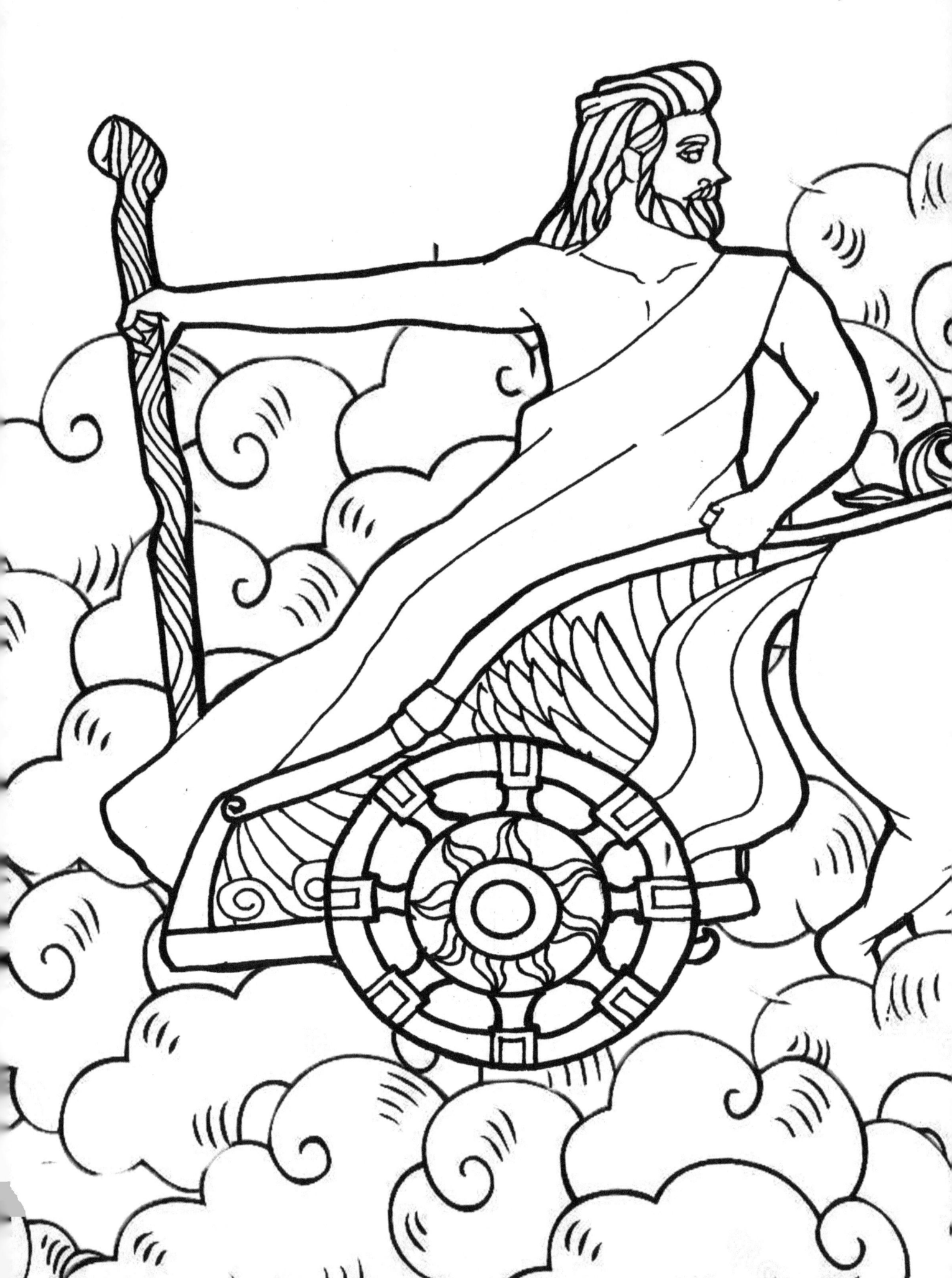

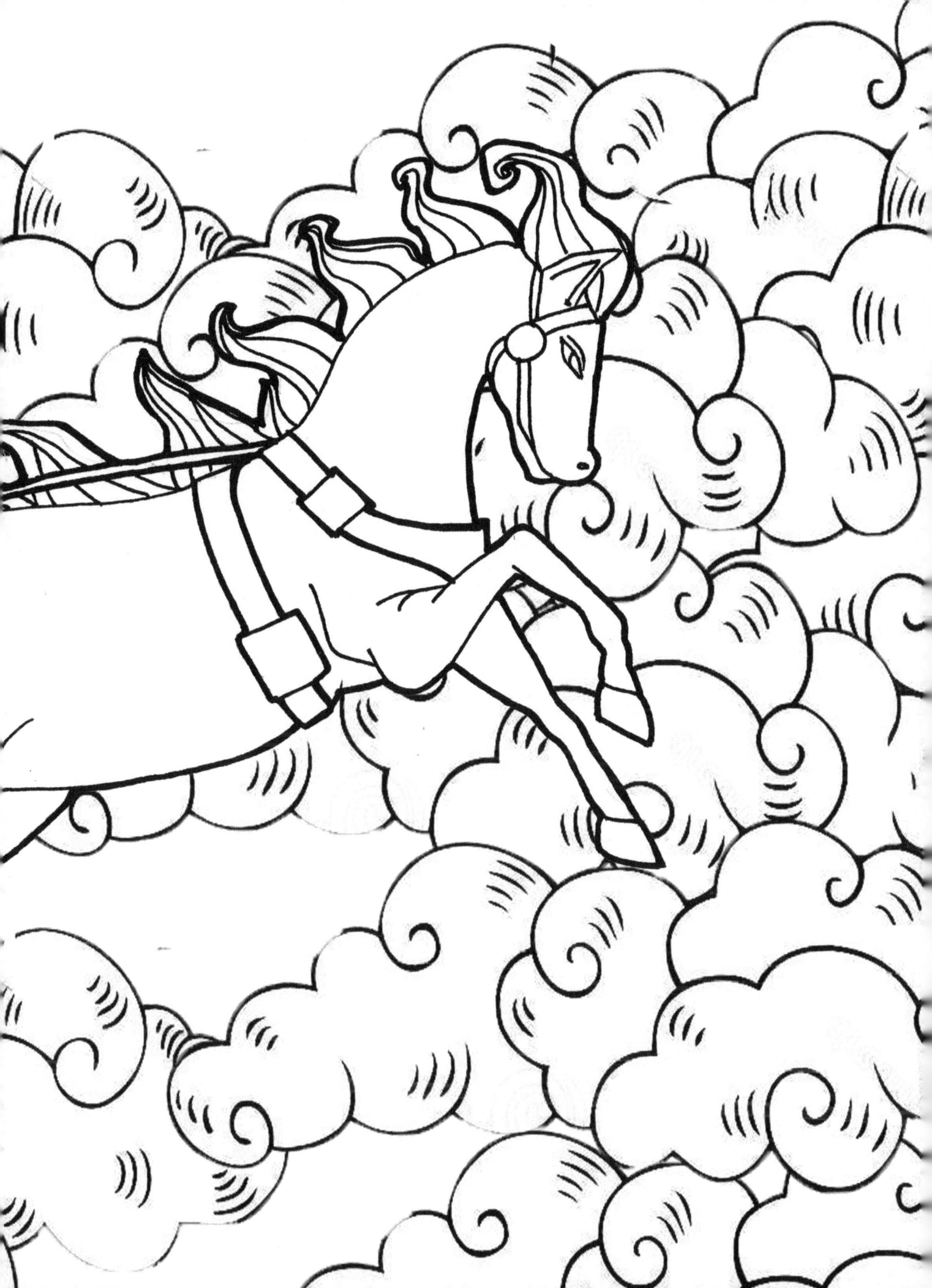

Gilgamesh and Enkidu

A Sumerian legend from Mesopotamia. Gilgamesh was
a warrior and a king while Enkidu lived in the forest
and had a more peaceful demeanor. They were good
friends and when Enkidu dies, Gilgamesh went in
search for a way to bring him back to life.

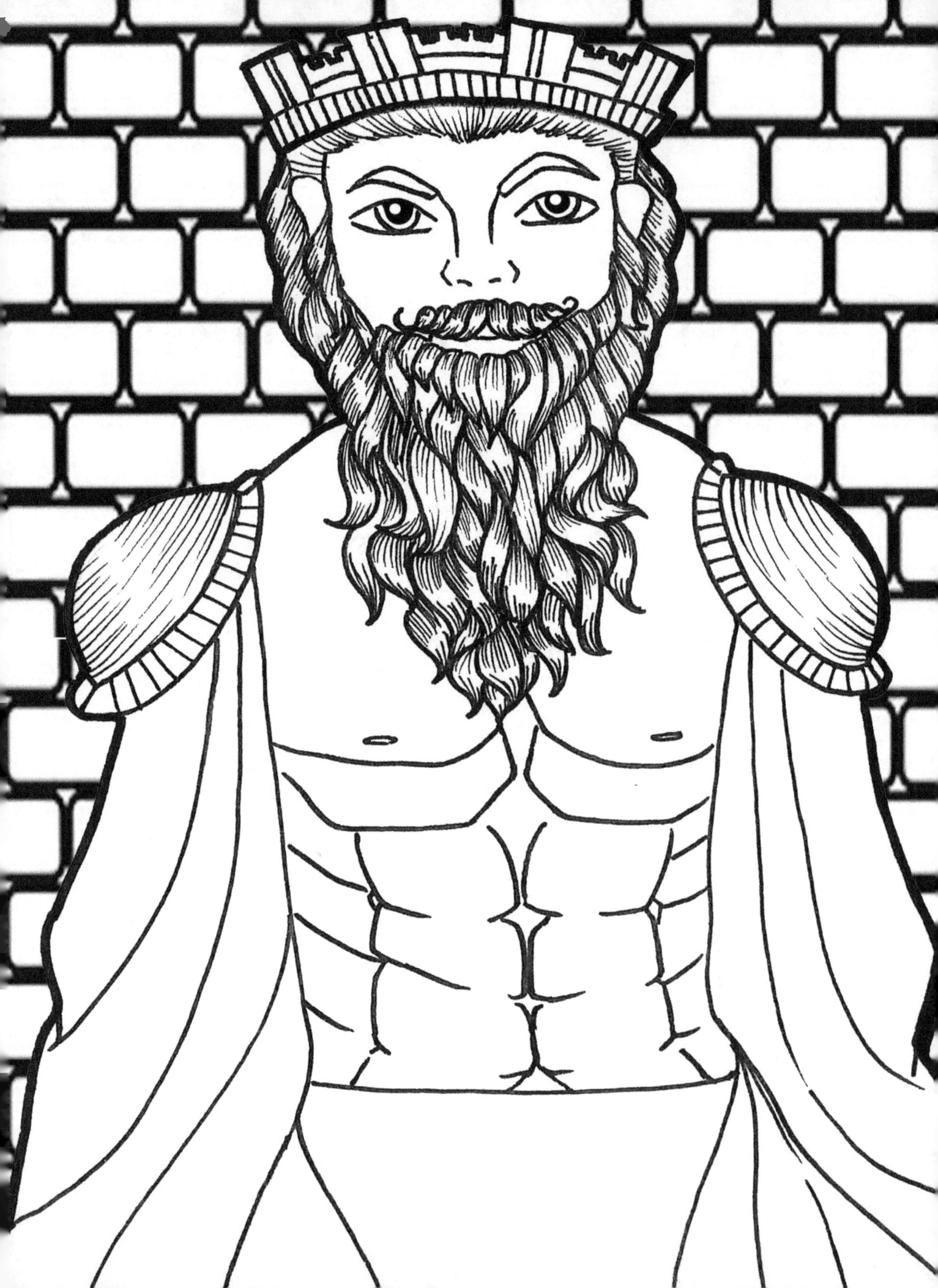

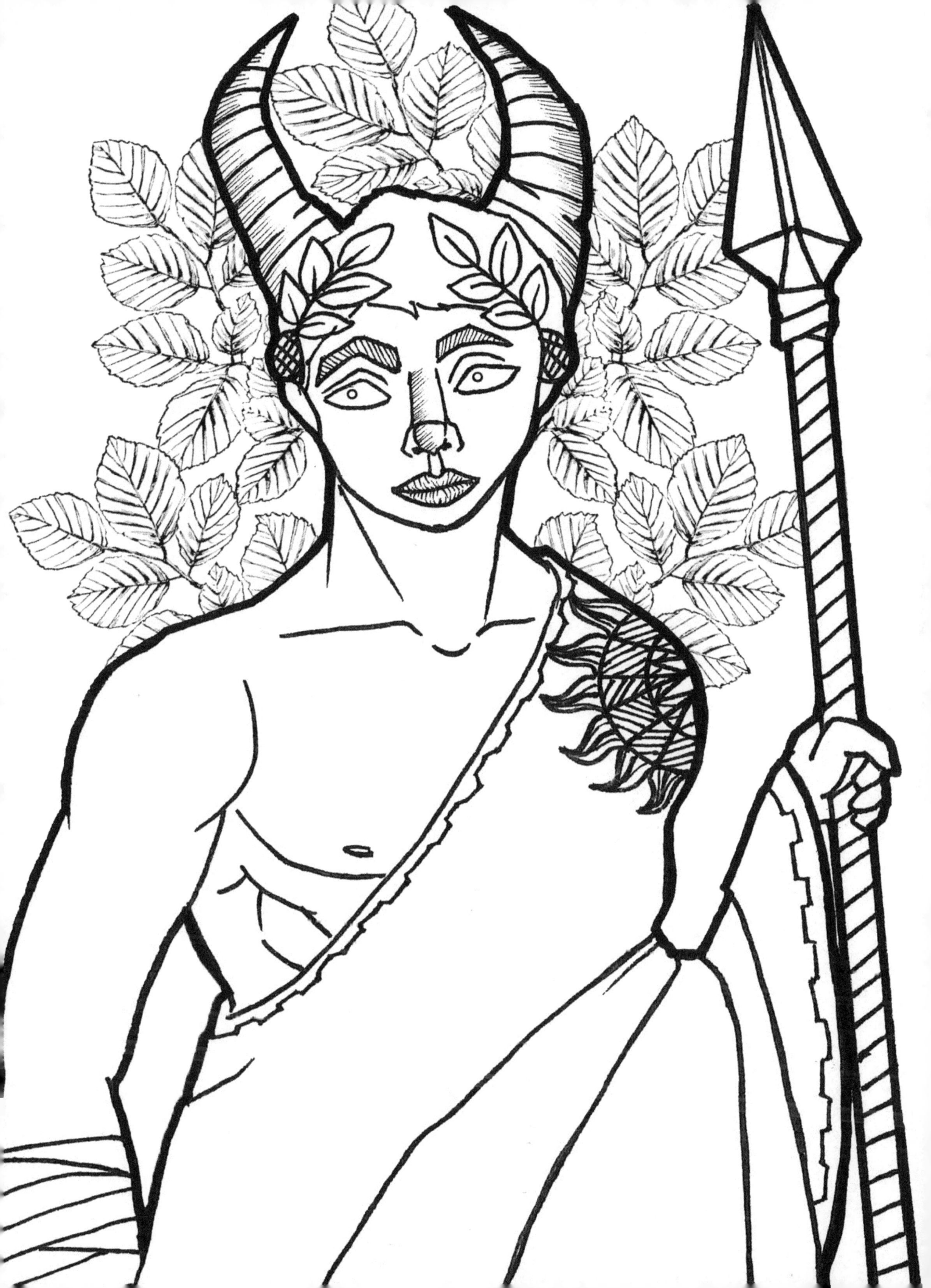

Cigwe'

The Thunderbird of American Indian mythology. Are considered to be very powerful, but are highly revered.

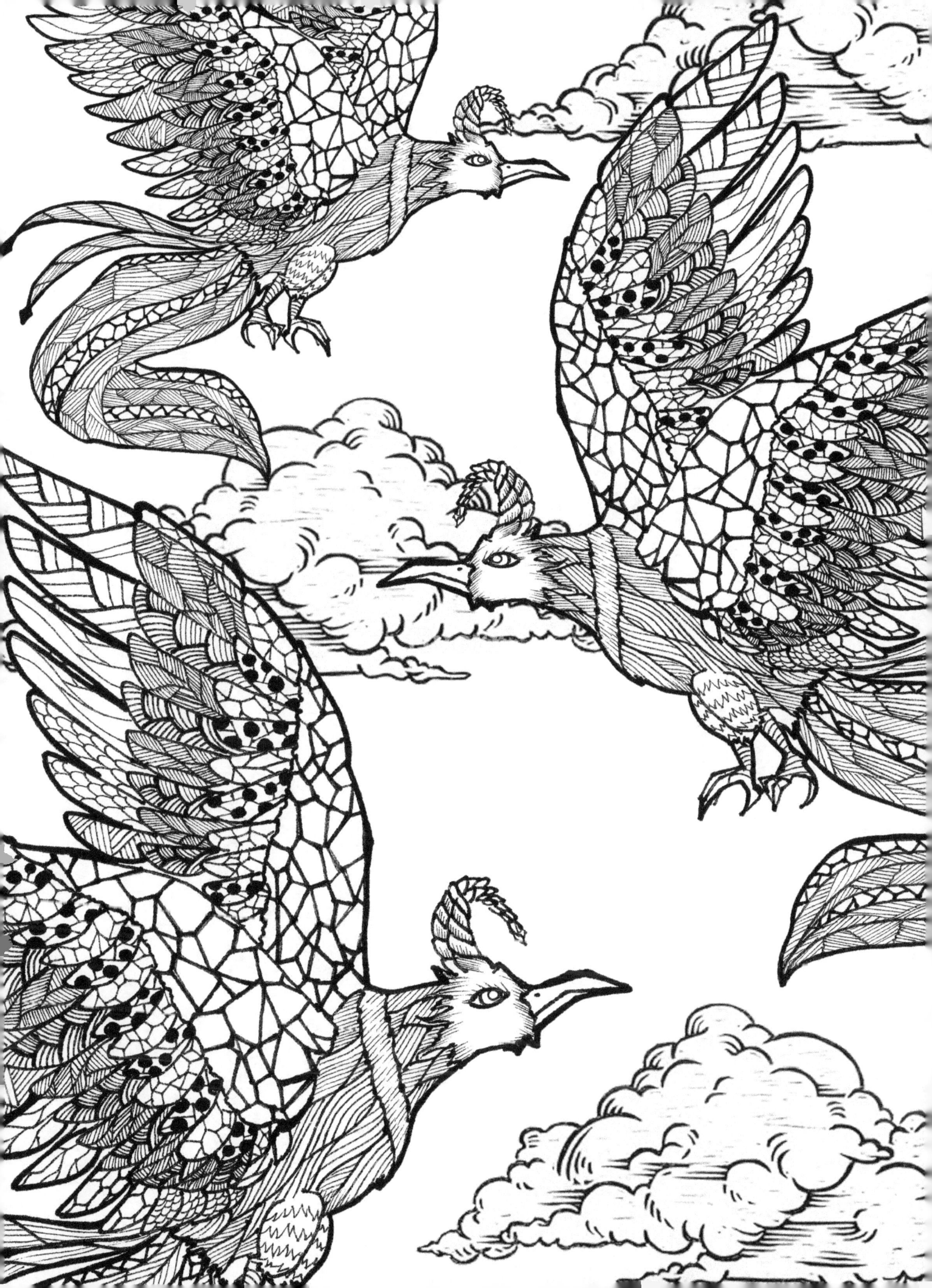

Mnito

Another American Indian legend. It is often depicted as a horned serpent and is an enemy of the Thunderbird.

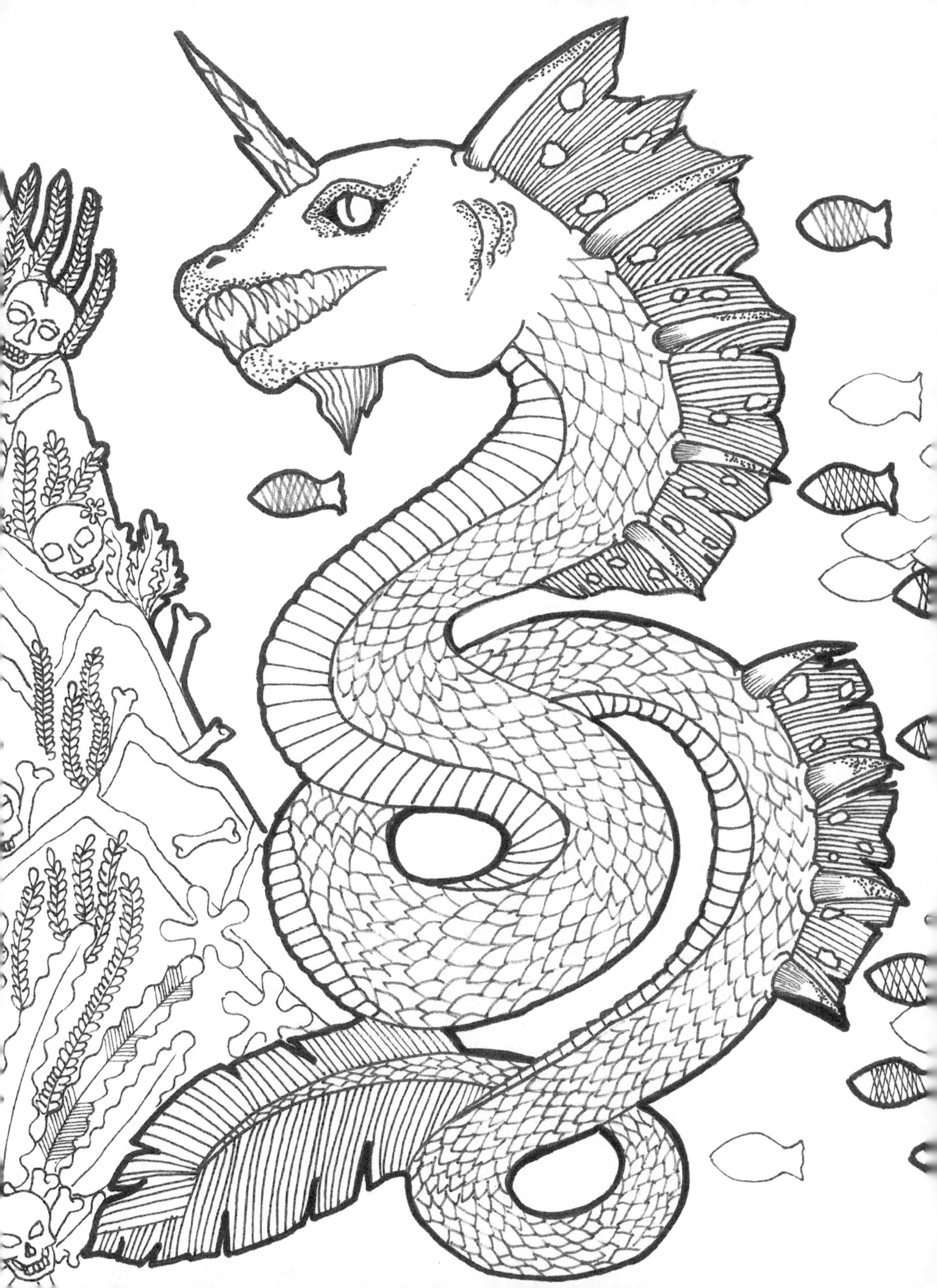

Coyote

Considered a trickster by the Comanche (Southern Plains Indians) and is best avoided.

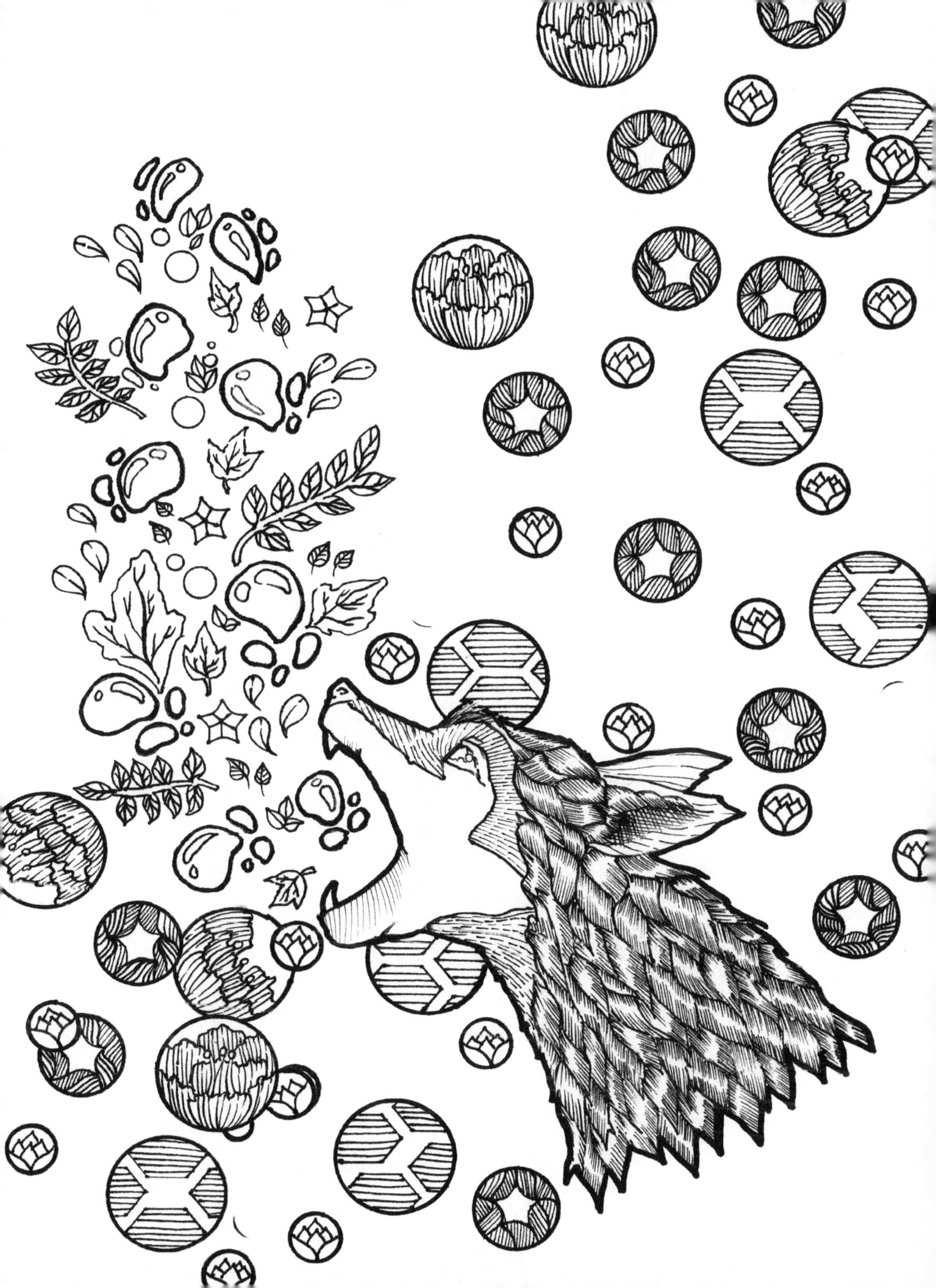

Story of the Northern Lights

The Northern Lights are well-known for the spectacular light show they give us in Canada and Alaska. According to an Eskimo legend the Aurora is produced by the torches of the spirits who lead recently departed souls to the afterlife.

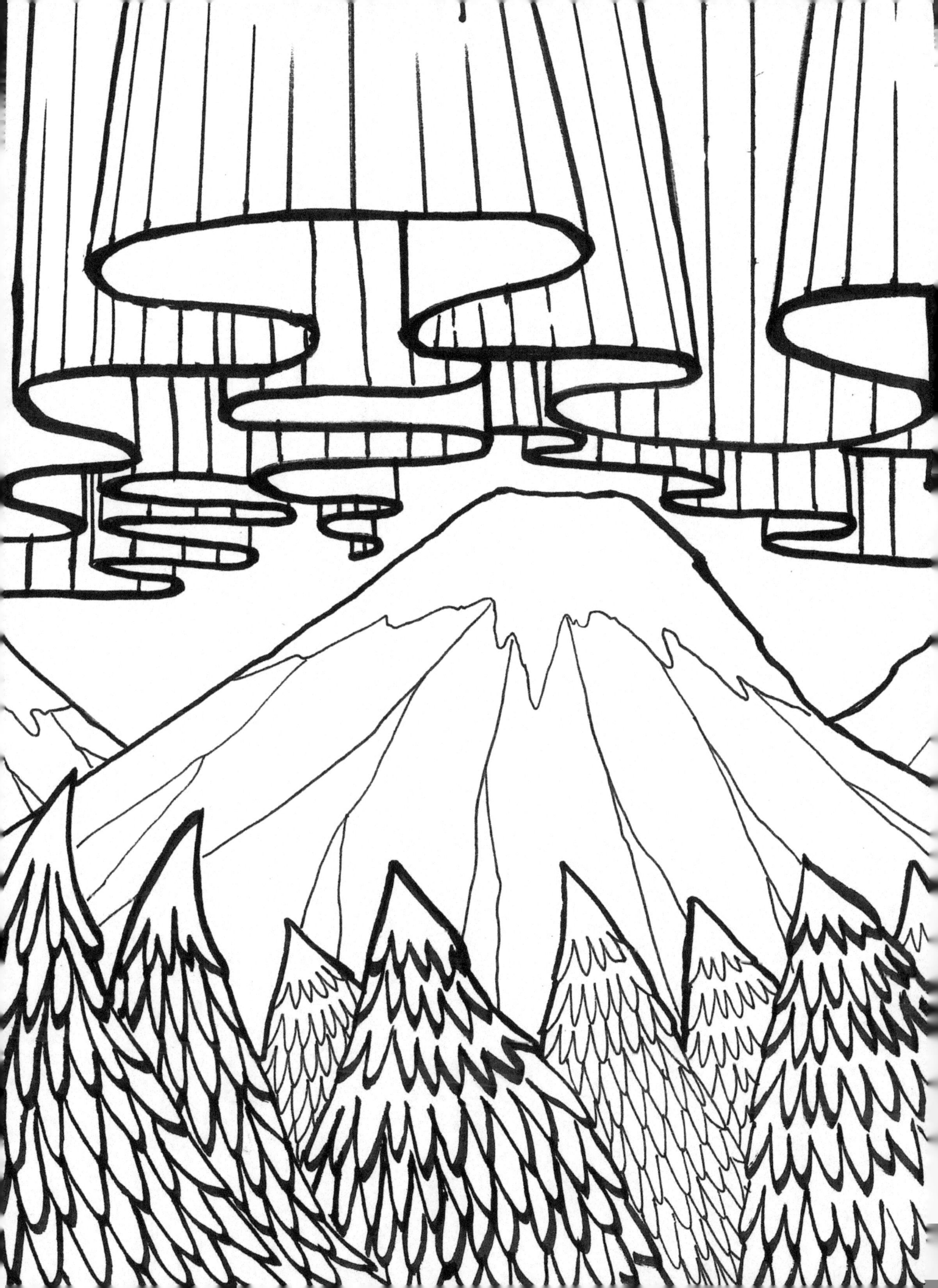

Shive

Originated in India and is the Hindu god of destruction.

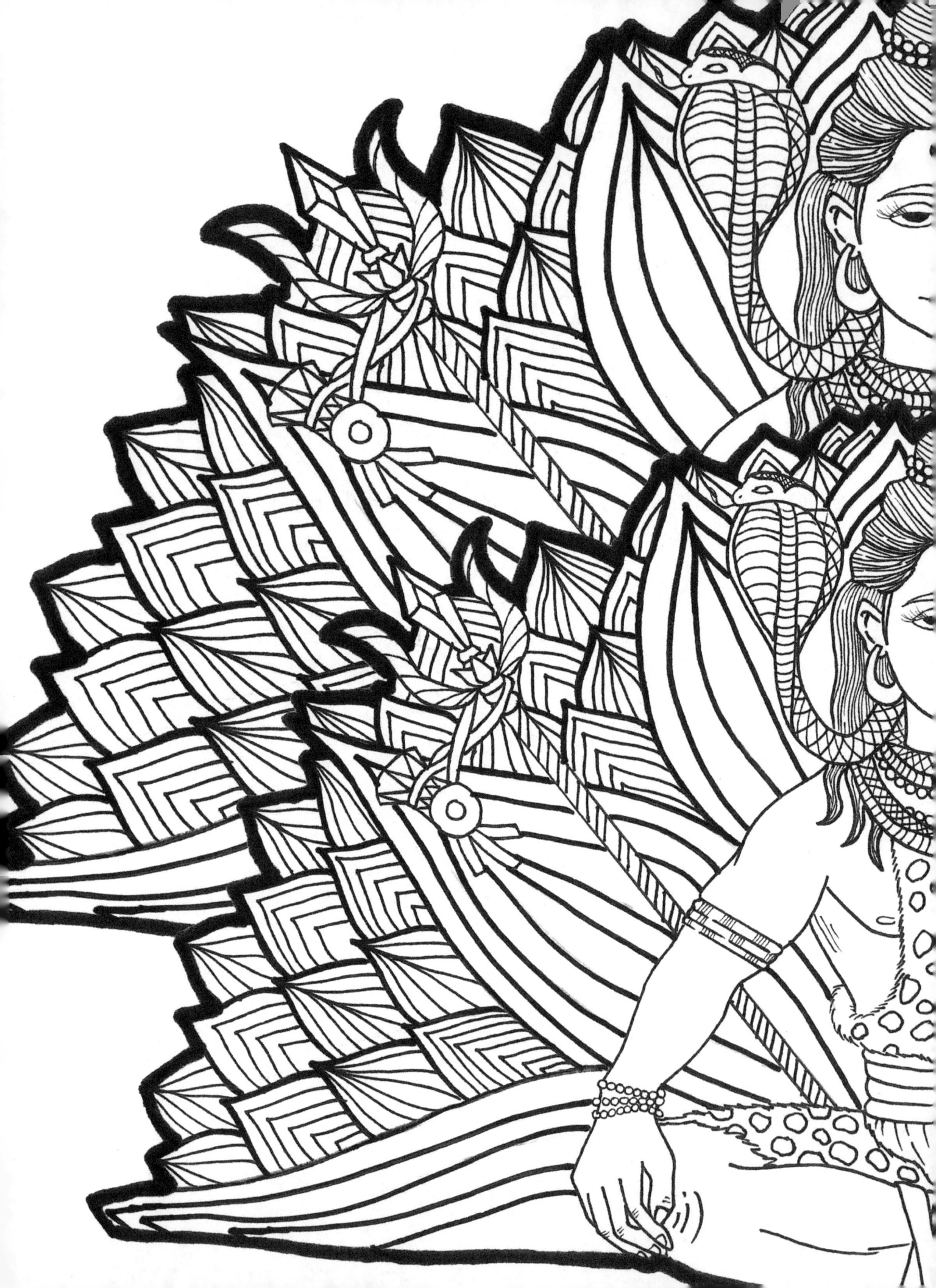

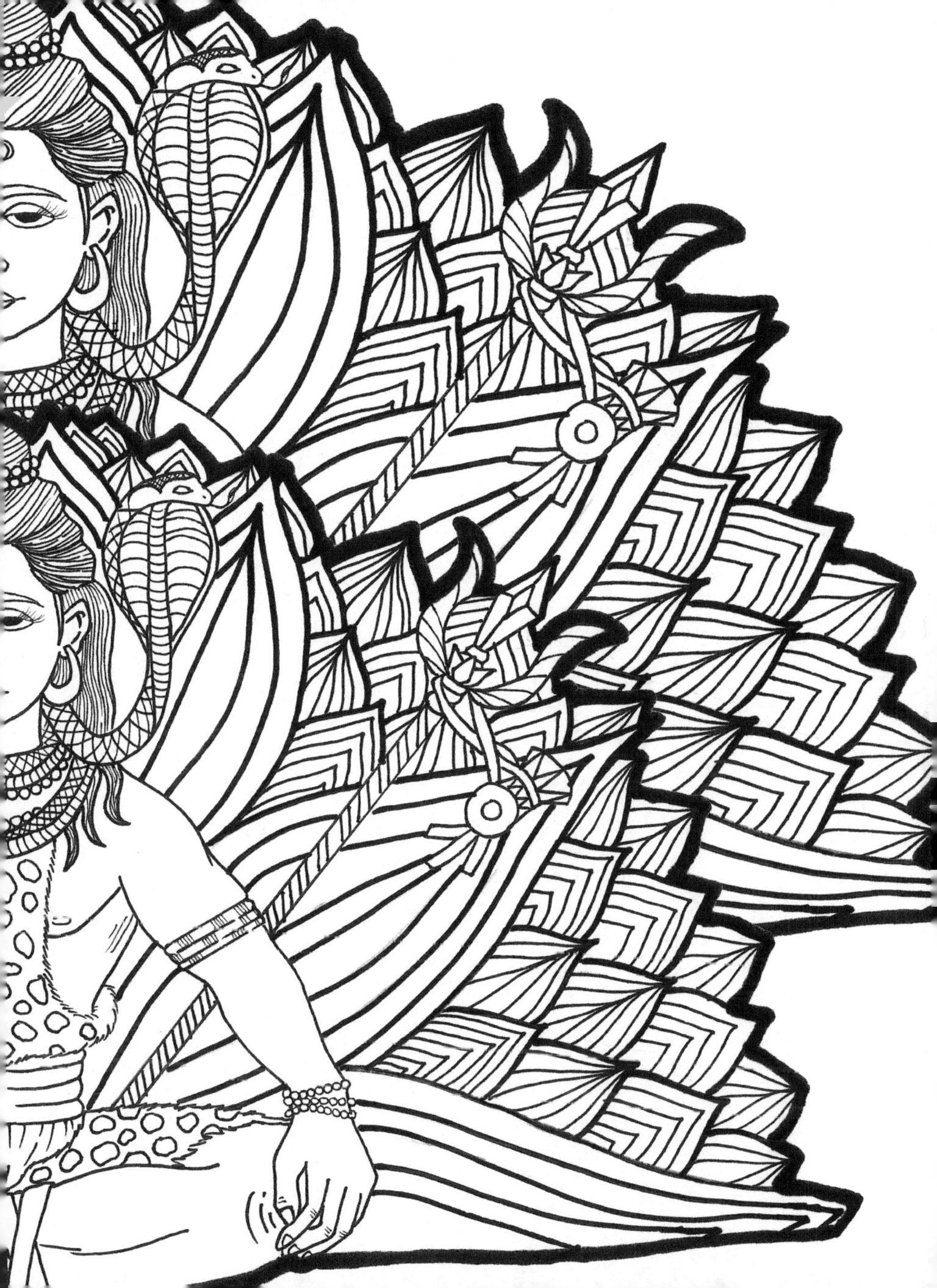

Bastet

Ancient Egyptian goddess of protection and cats.

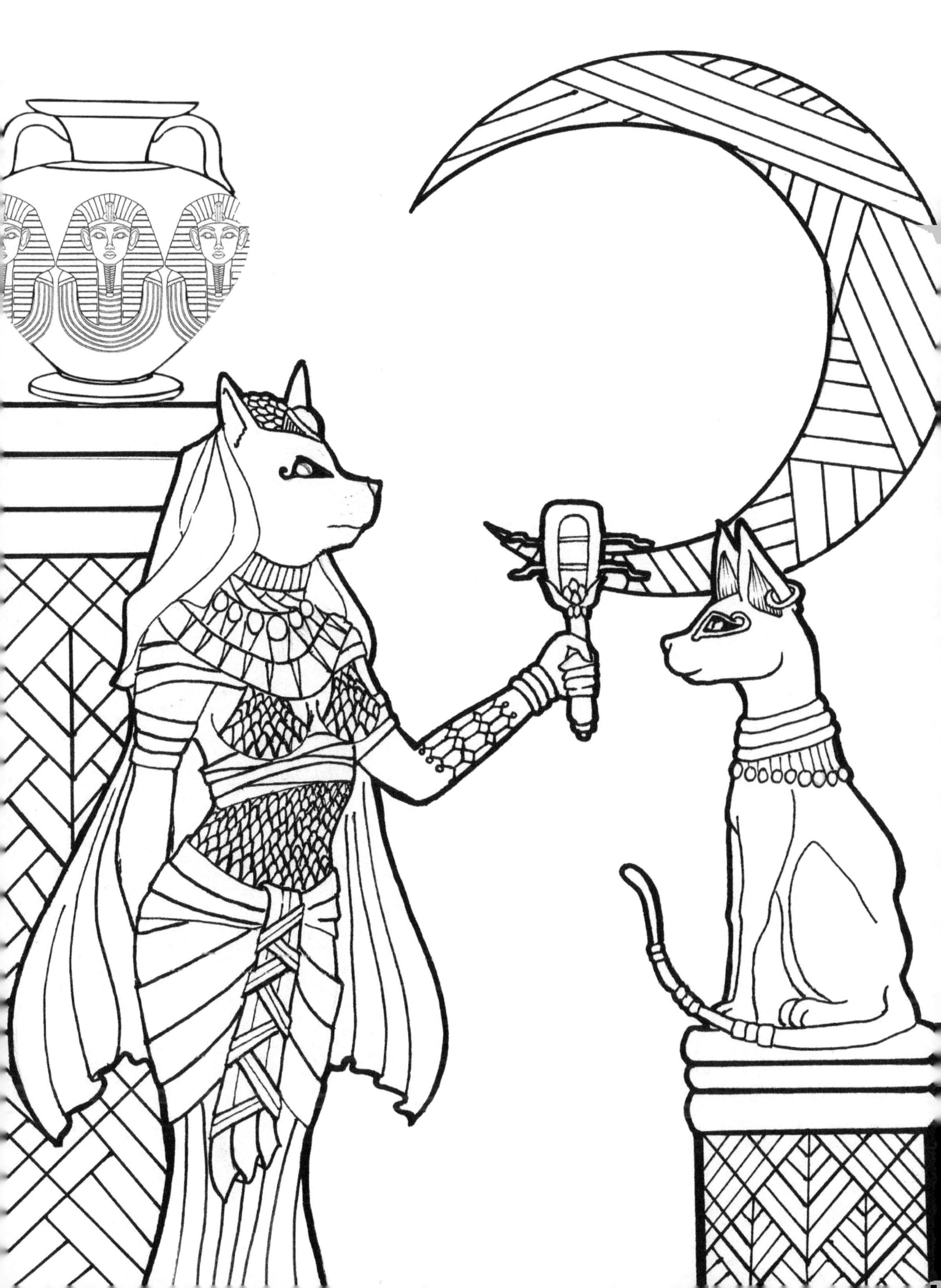

The Gandharvas

In Hinduism, they are male servants who are heavenly musicians and servants of Indra. India in origin.

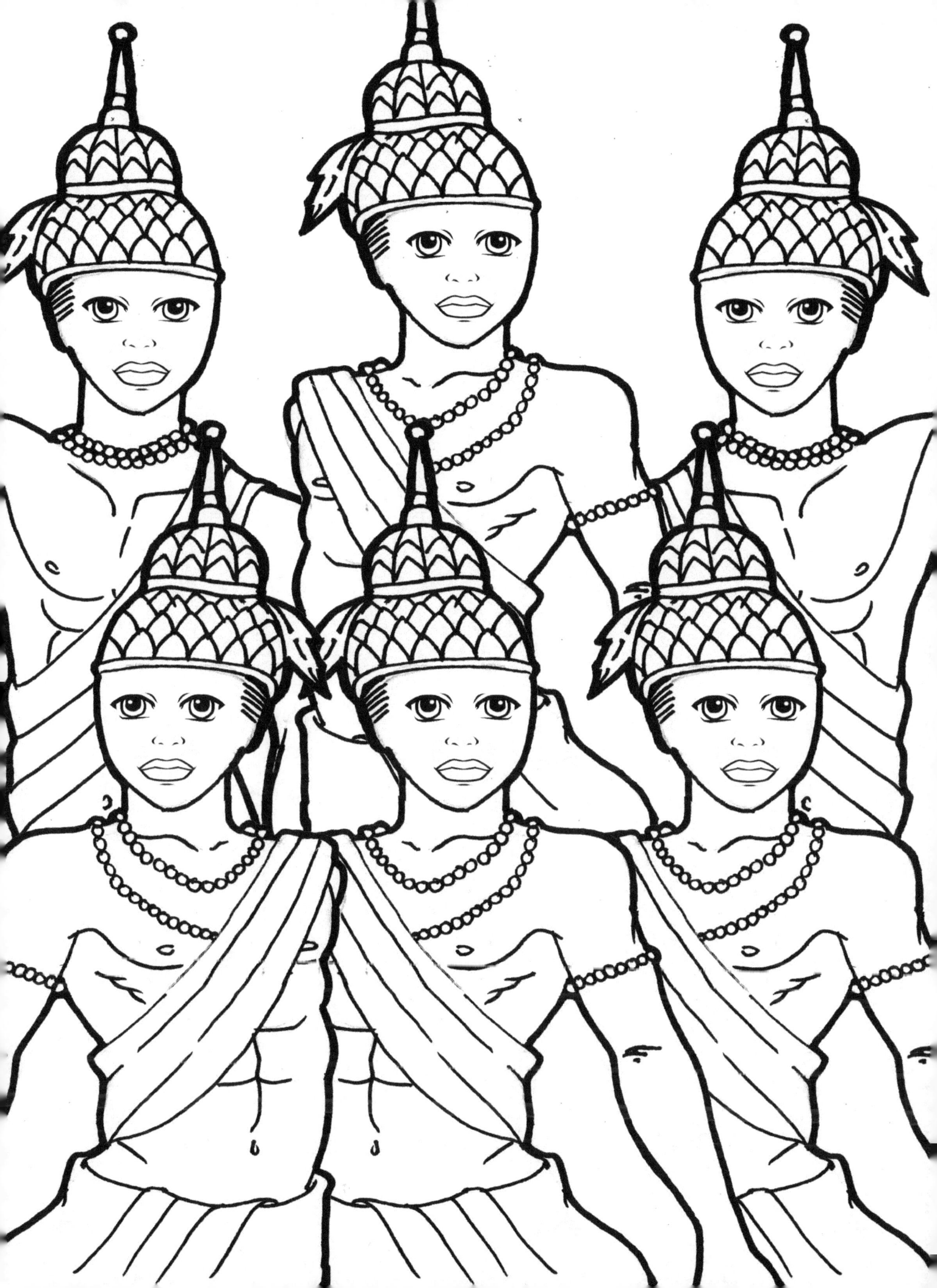

Kanaloa

The Hawaiian god of the underworld and a teacher of magic.

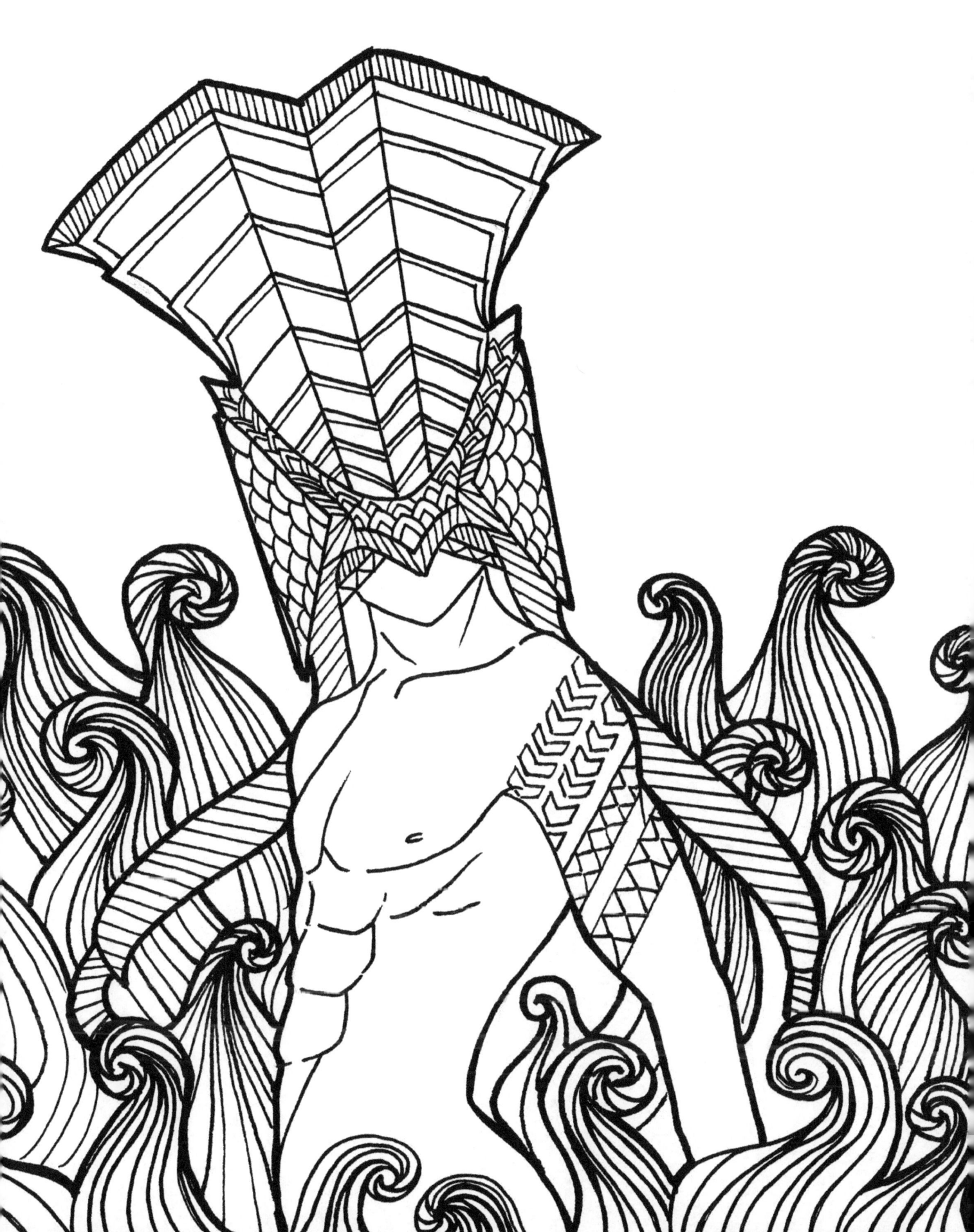

Fionn

Scottish or Pictish in origin. He is a magician, warrior, and a poet.

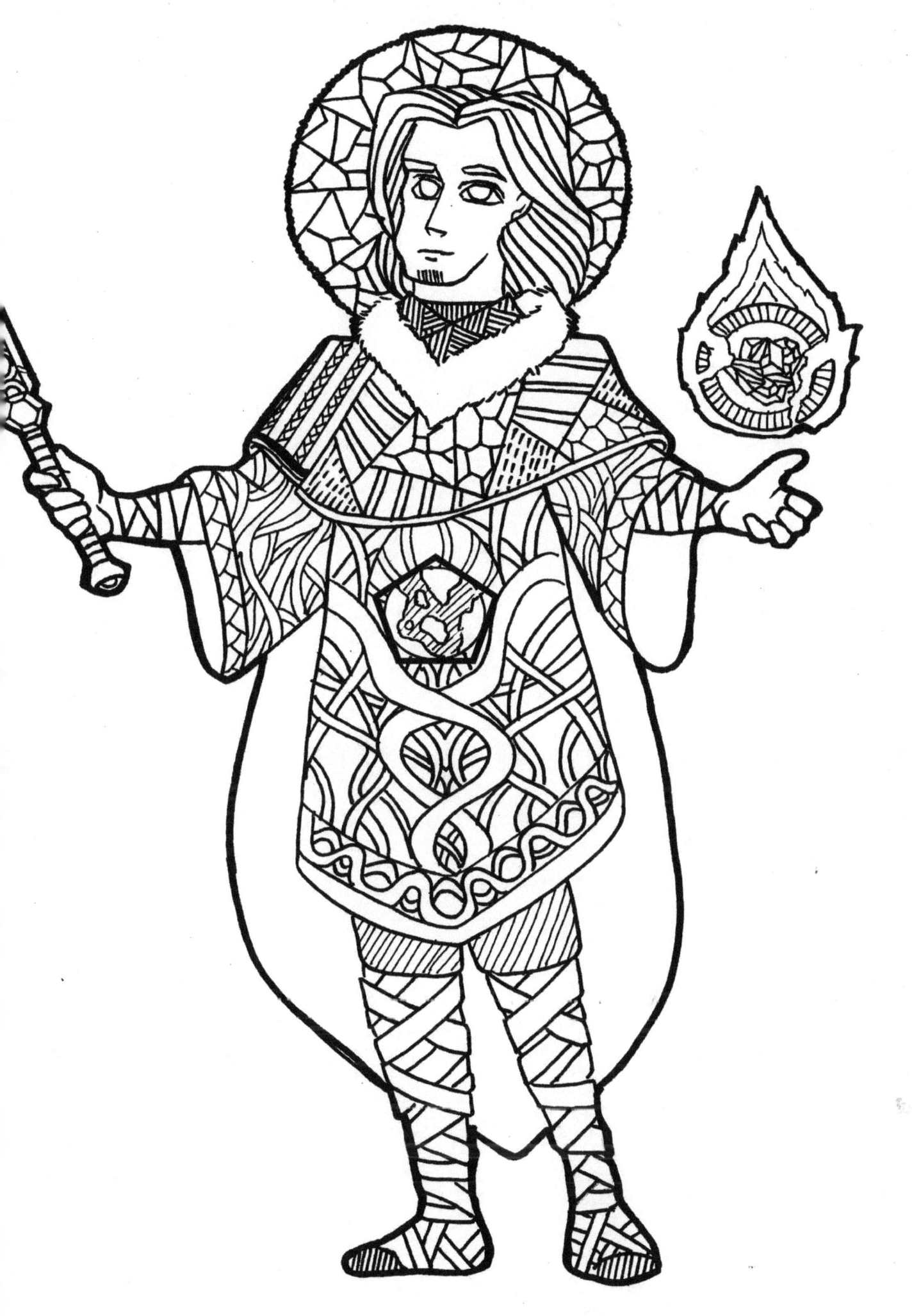

Joro-Gumo

Japanese in origin, Joro-Gumo is a spider woman who disguises herself as a beautiful lady to seduce men, after which she wraps them in her web, poisons them, and eats them.

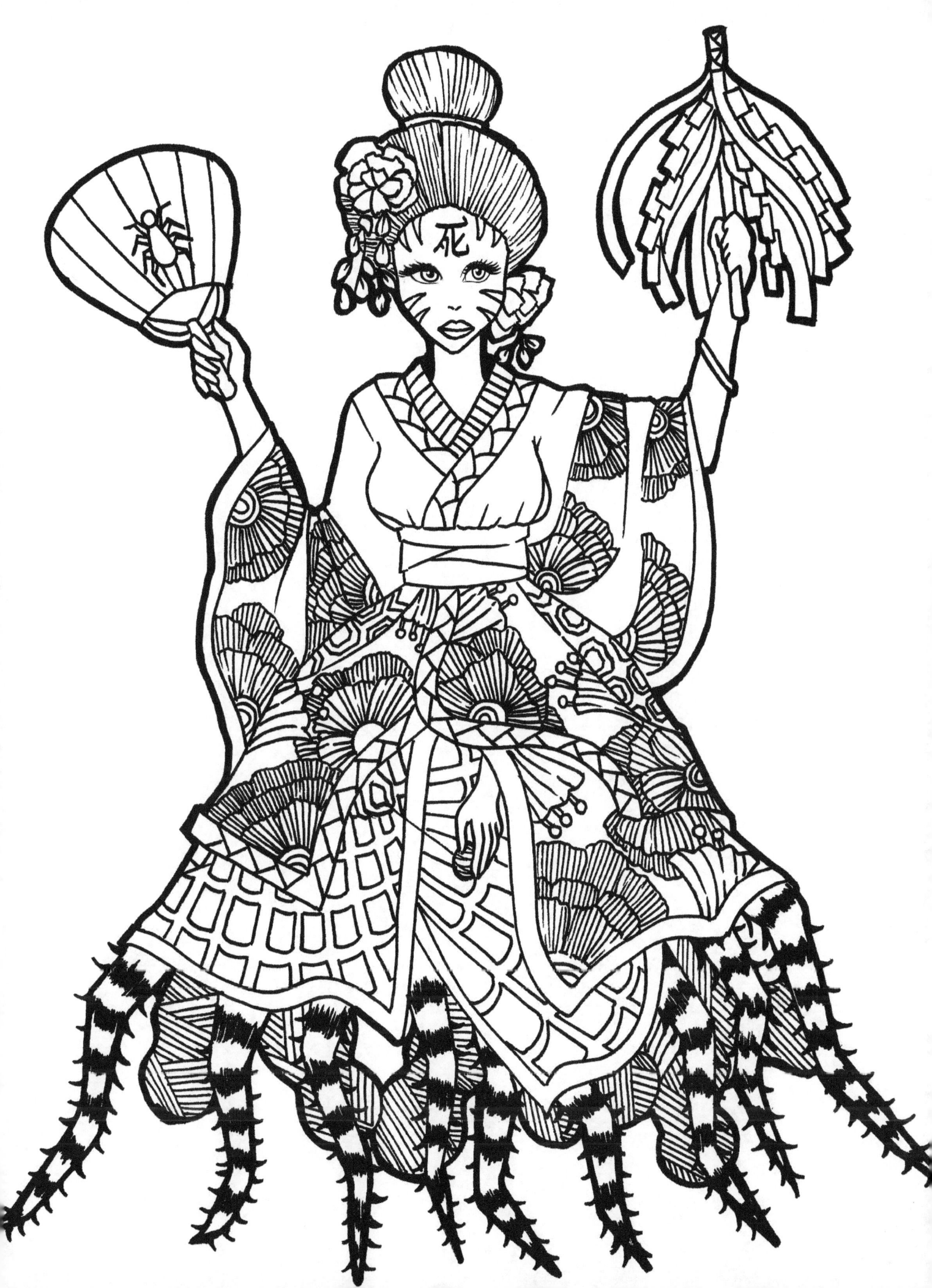

Kylin

Chinese in origin, The Kylin is considered an animal of longevity, living for two millennia,. In ancient China, it was believed to dictate the rise and fall of a dynasty.

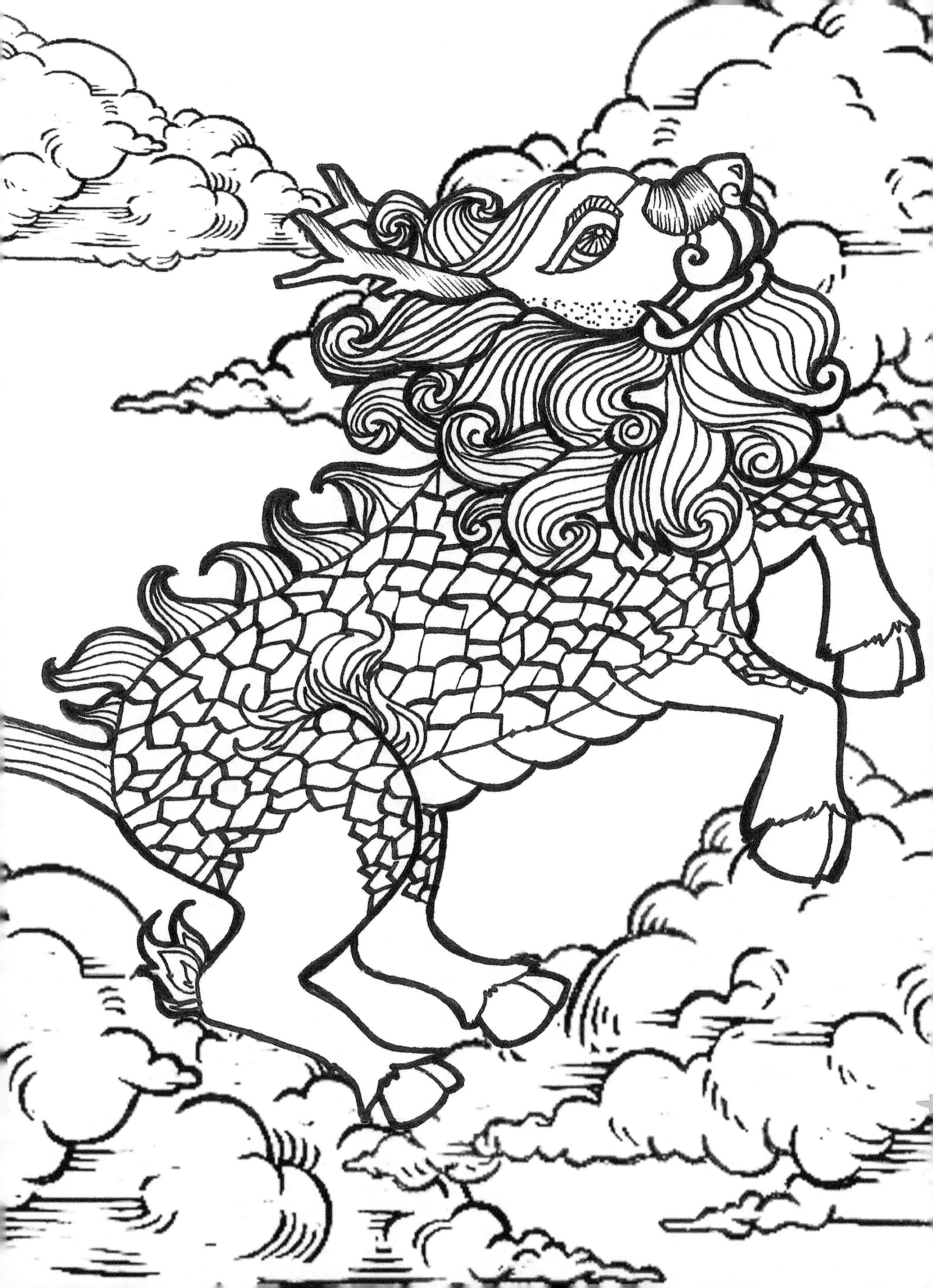

The Phoenix

The phoenix is believed to be Greek in origin and is a bird that symbolizes eternal life or renewal. Upon it's death, it is believed to either build a pyre of cinnamon twigs where it sits upon it and lights itself on fire, or bursts into flames only to be reborn from the ashes.

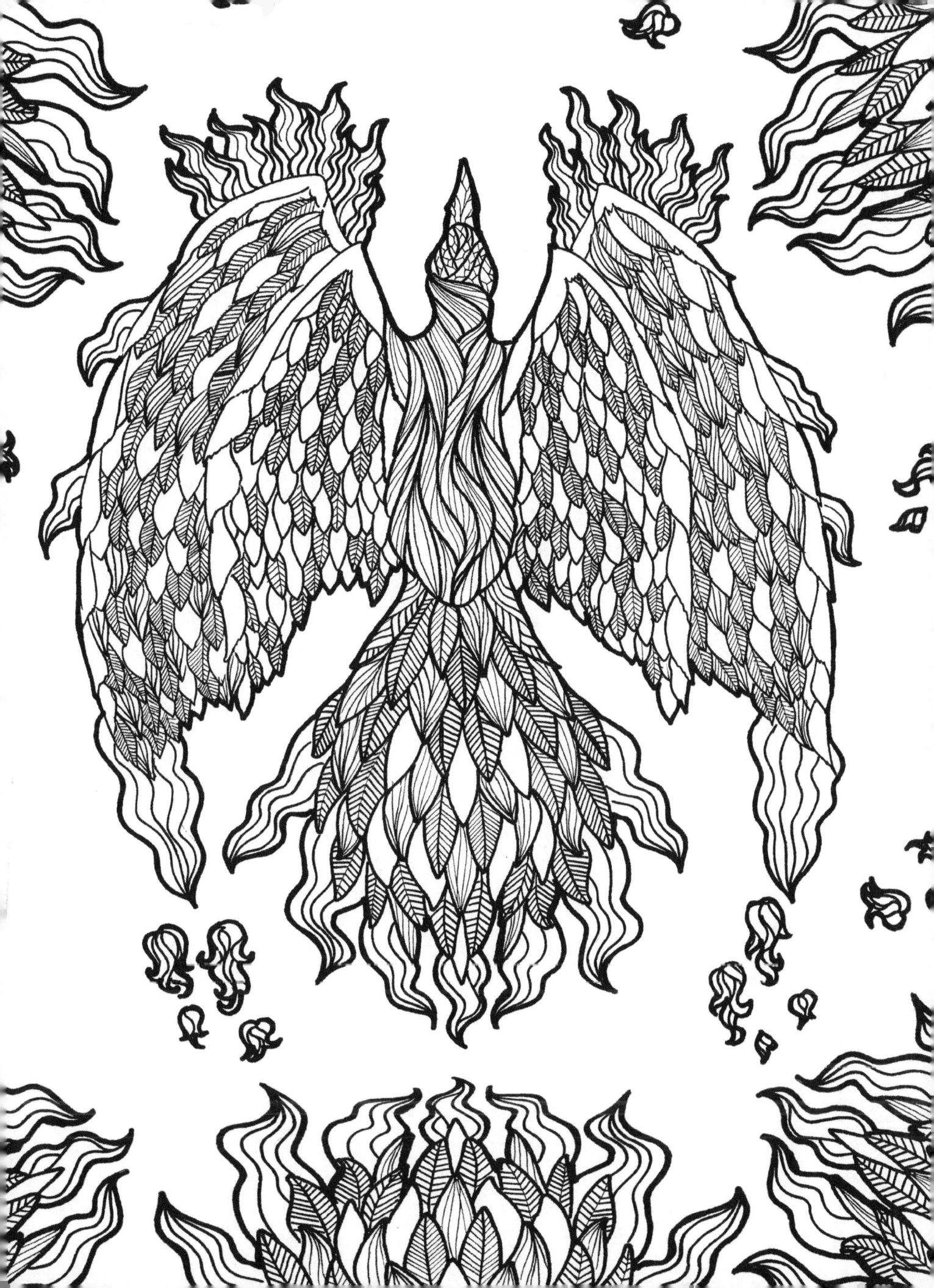

Snarly Yowl

A legend in West Virginia (USA), the Snarly Yowl is a dog-like creature that roams the mountain area of Harper's Ferry. It is said to appear and vanish instantly, challenging any who travel the older main roads of the Blue Ridge and South Mountain, a series of mountains that stretch through Virginia, West Virginia, and Maryland.

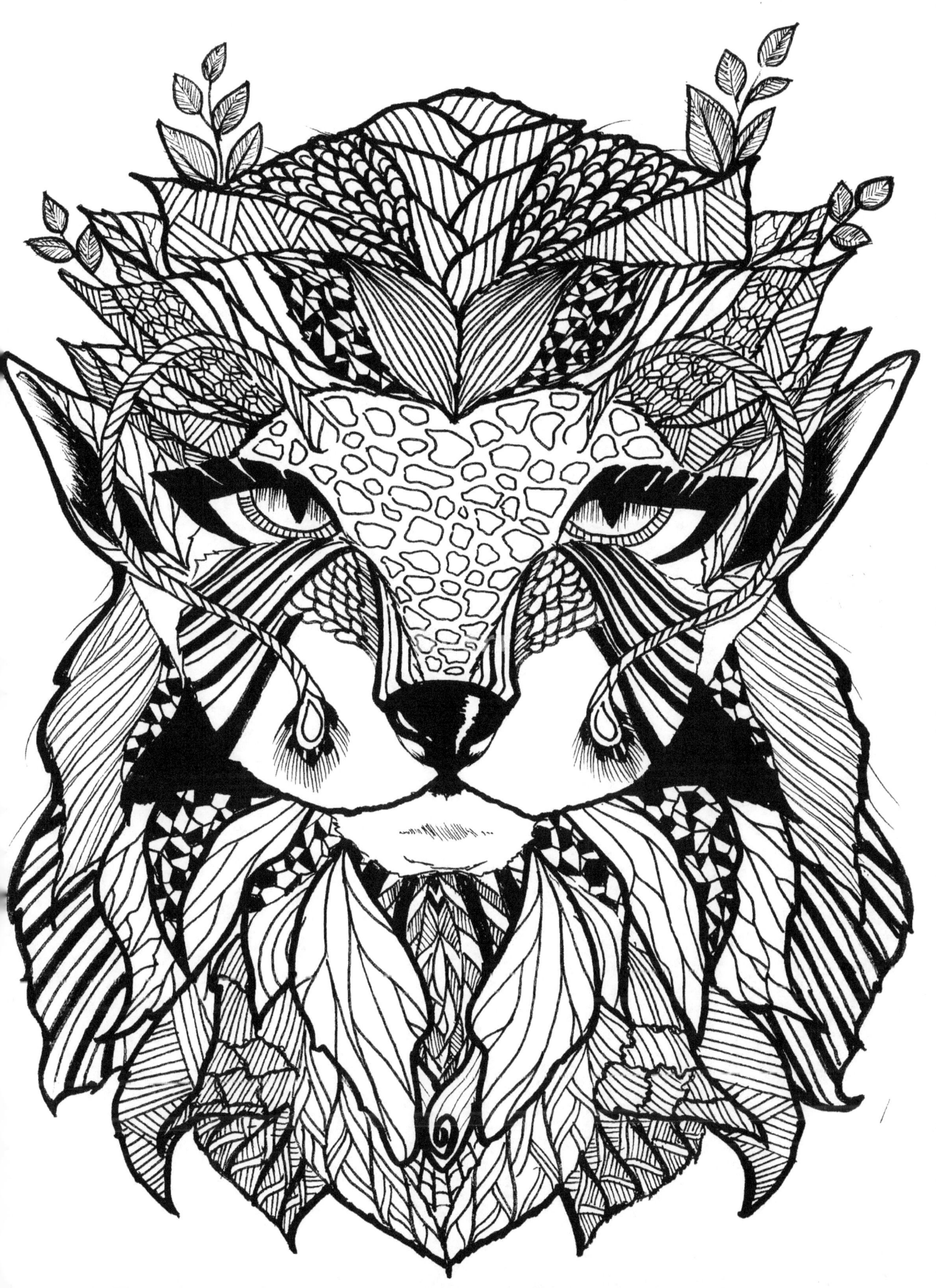

Legend of Devil's Tower

This is an American Indian legend that originates in Wyoming (USA). According to the story, bears roamed the area. One day, some girls were playing when a bear chased them back home to their village. They jumped on a rock and pleaded with the rock to save them. The rock took pity on them and rose into the sky with the bear jumping at it and tearing at it with its claws, the marks of which can still be seen today. The girls are believed to have become the seven stars in the sky, known as the Pleiades, which can be seen clearly in the Wyoming sky.

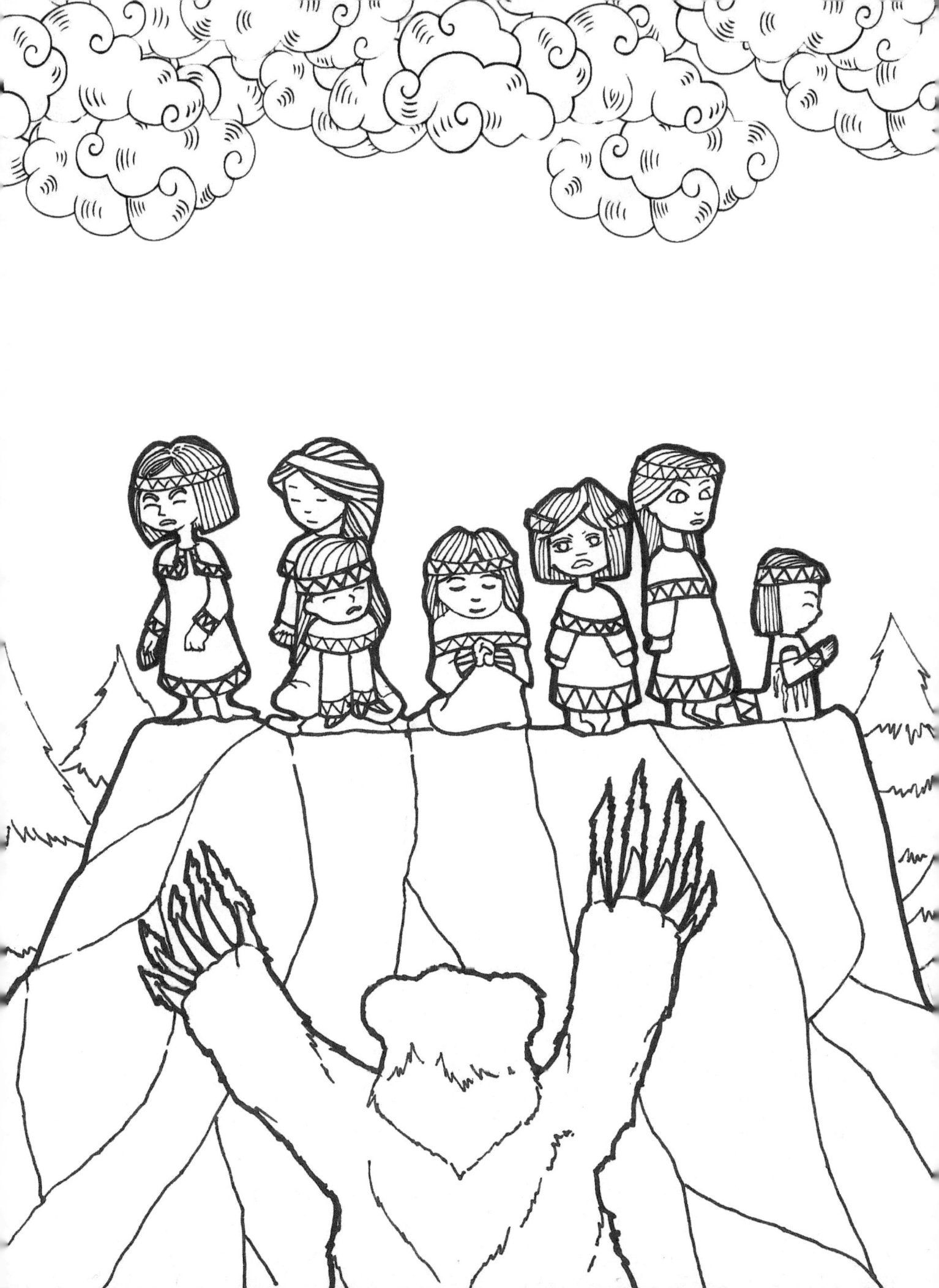

Quetzalcoatl

Though showcased in many Mesoamerica architecture and art, Quetzalcoatl is considered the Aztec god of civilization and learning. He is credited with bringing civilization and knowledge to humanity.

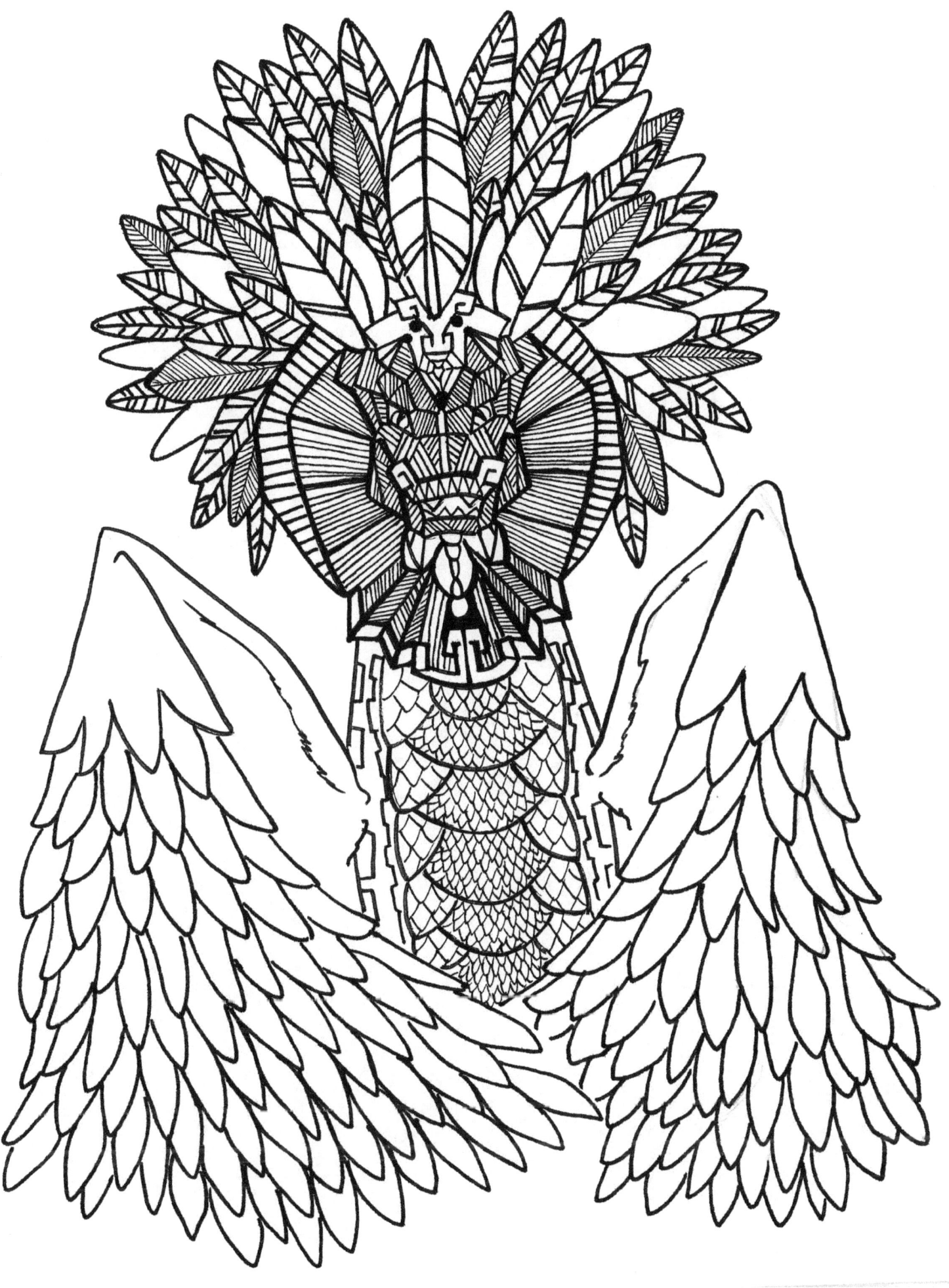

More in the Adult Coloring Book series...

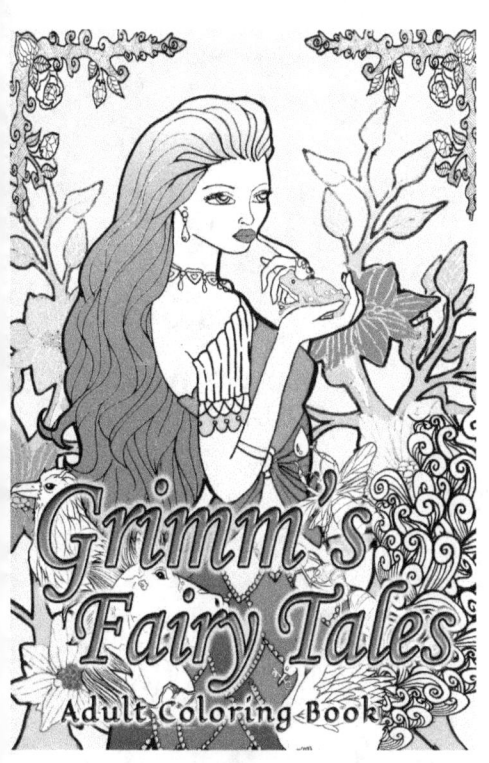

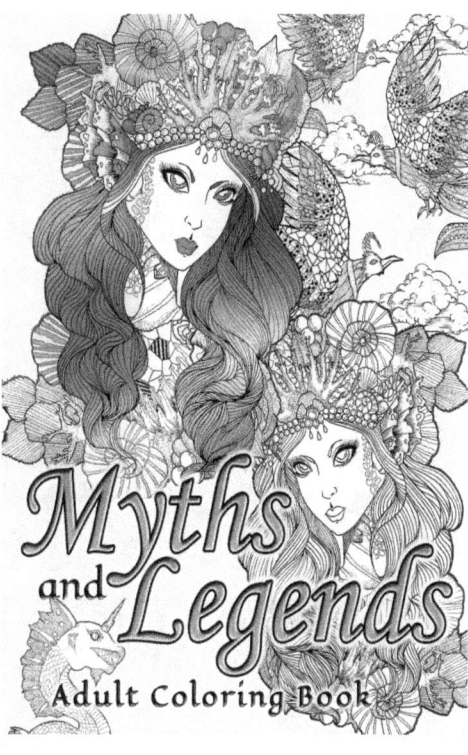

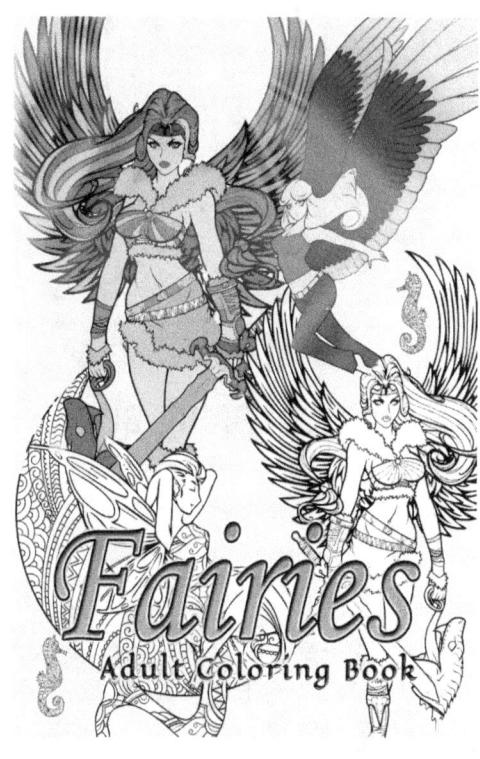

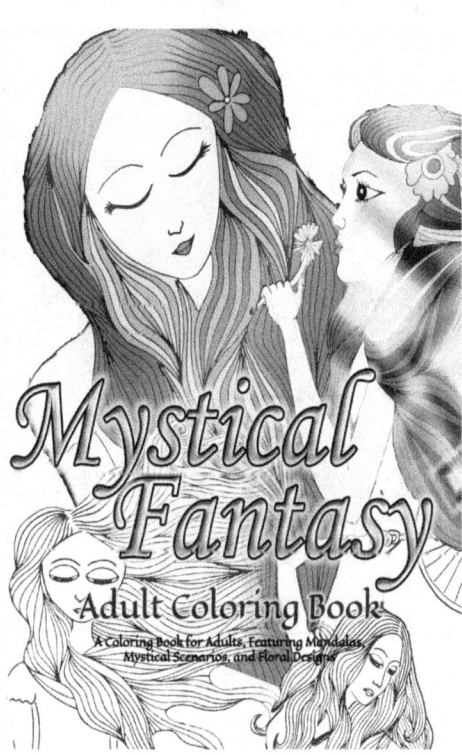

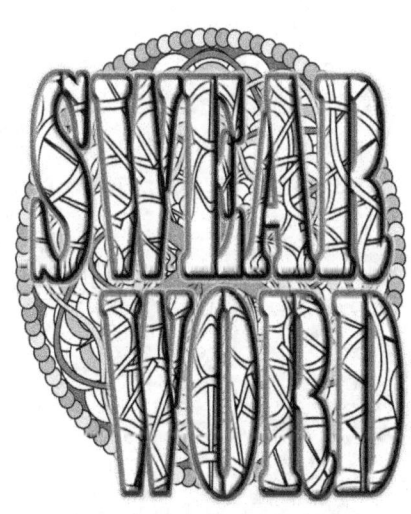

ADULT COLORING BOOK

RELAX WITH CURSE WORDS

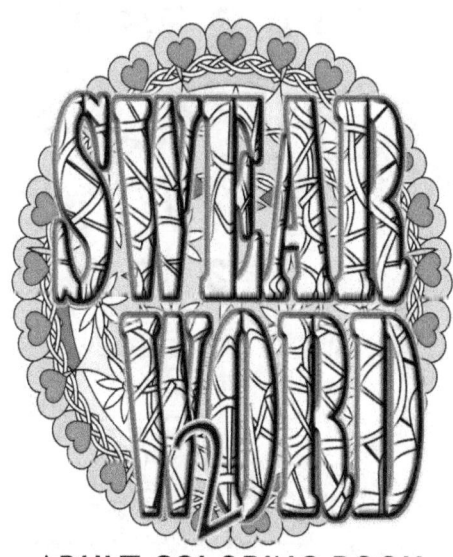

ADULT COLORING BOOK

RELAX WITH CURSE WORDS

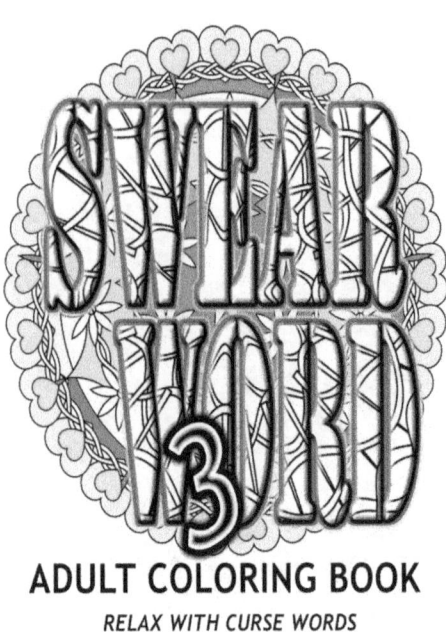

SWEAR WORD 3

ADULT COLORING BOOK

RELAX WITH CURSE WORDS

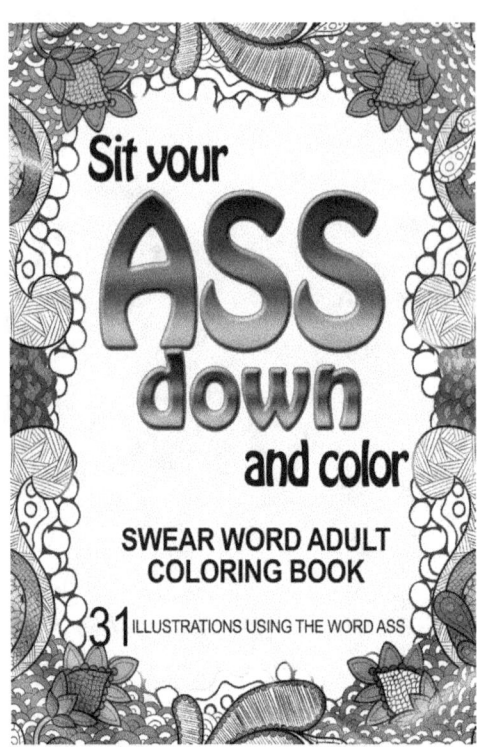

Sit your
ASS
down
and color

SWEAR WORD ADULT
COLORING BOOK

31 ILLUSTRATIONS USING THE WORD ASS

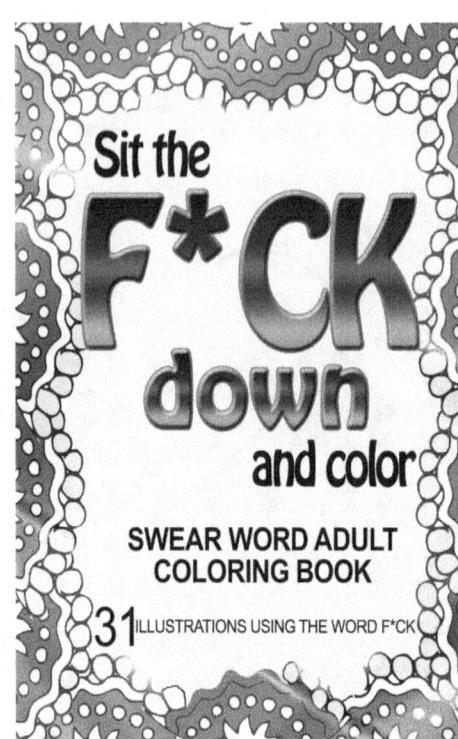

Sit the
F*CK
down
and color

SWEAR WORD ADULT
COLORING BOOK

31 ILLUSTRATIONS USING THE WORD F*CK

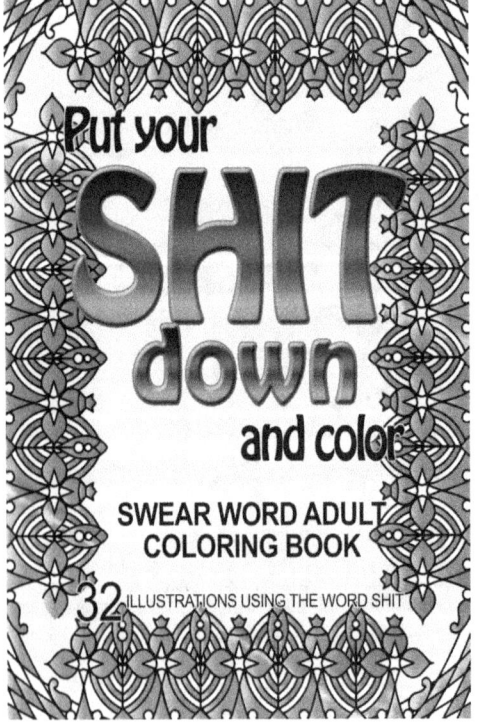

Put your
SHIT
down
and color

SWEAR WORD ADULT
COLORING BOOK

32 ILLUSTRATIONS USING THE WORD SHIT

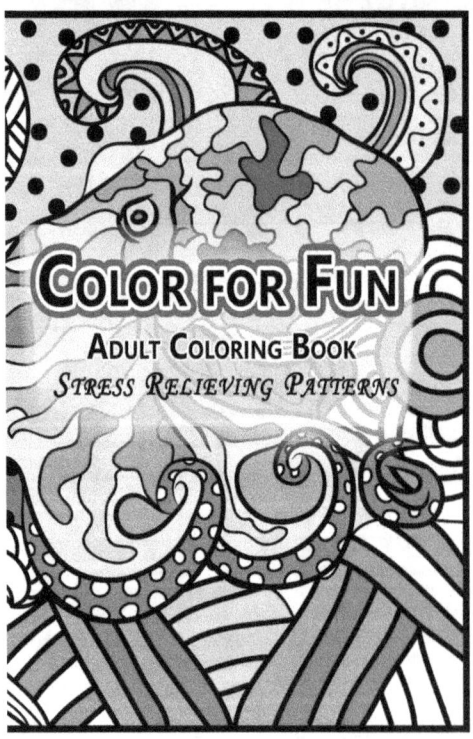

COLOR FOR FUN
ADULT COLORING BOOK
STRESS RELIEVING PATTERNS

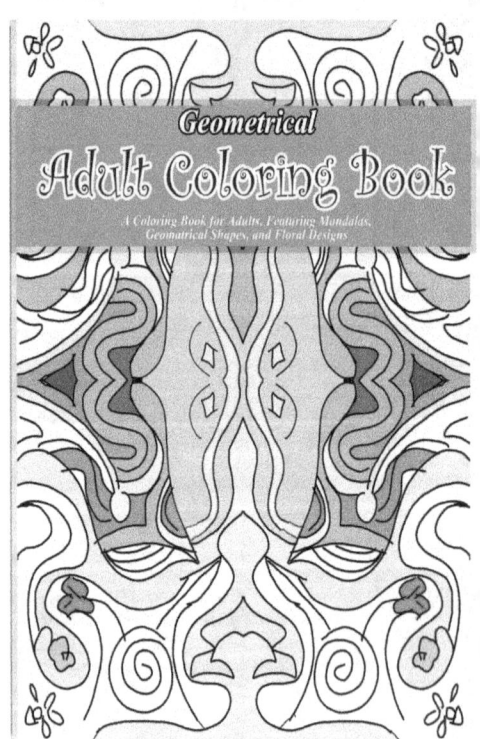

Geometrical
Adult Coloring Book
*A Coloring Book for Adults, Featuring Mandalas,
Geometrical Shapes, and Floral Designs*

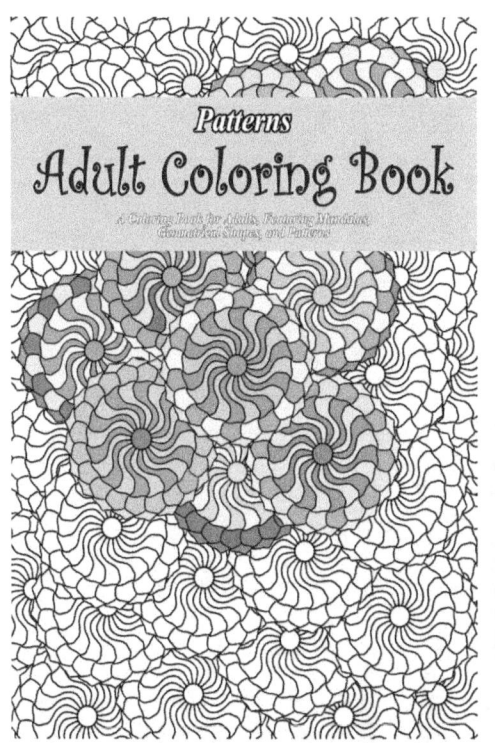

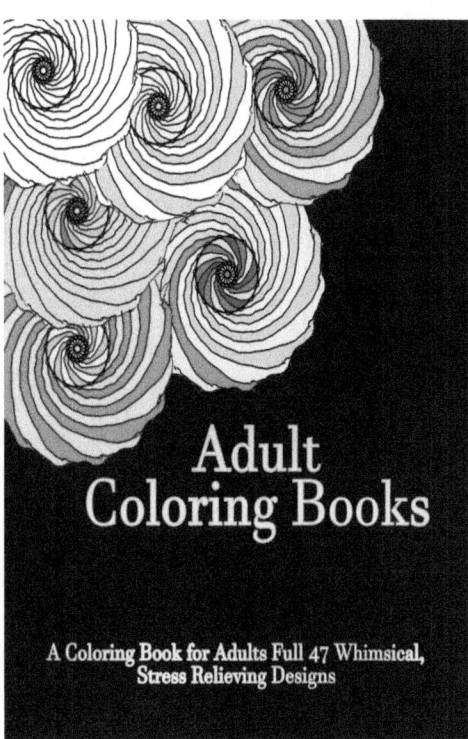

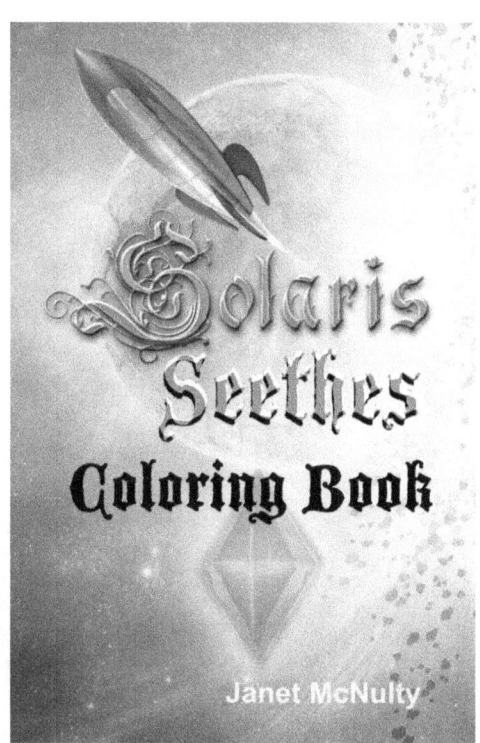

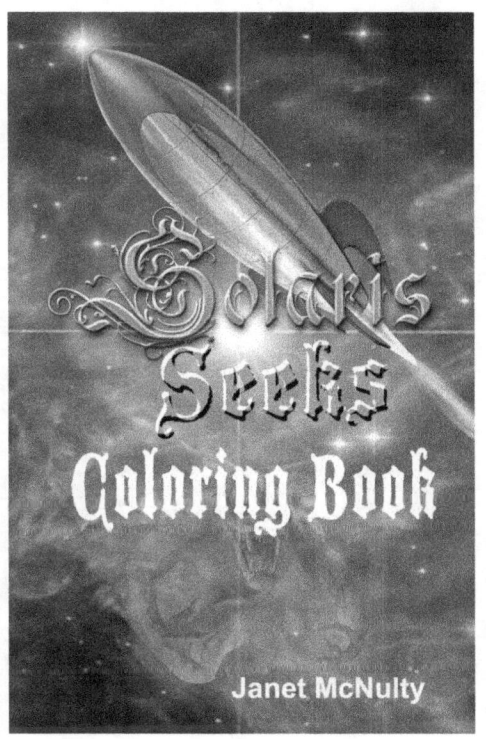

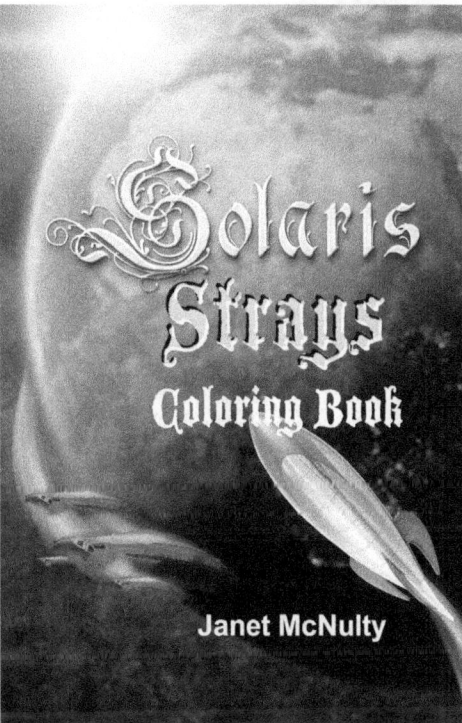

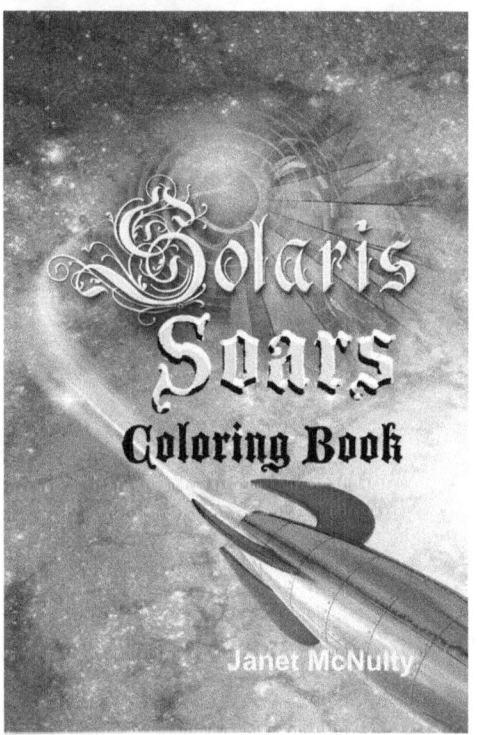

www.ingramcontent.com/pod-product-compliance
Lightning Source LLC
Chambersburg PA
CBHW080700190526
45169CB00006B/2196